Southern Indians and Anthropologists

Southern Indians and Anthropologists

CULTURE, POLITICS, AND IDENTITY

Edited by Lisa J. Lefler and Frederic W. Gleach

Southern Anthropological Society Proceedings, No. 35
Michael V. Angrosino, Series Editor

The University of Georgia Press
Athens and London

Southern Anthropological Society
Founded 1966

OFFICERS, 2000–2001
Mark Moberg, President
David Johnson, Past-President
Barbara Hendry, President-Elect
Melissa Schrift, Secretary-Treasurer
Mark Moberg, Councilor
John Studstill, Councilor
Melinda Bollar Wagner, Councilor

Program Coordinator, 2000
Lisa J. Lefler

Published by the University of Georgia Press
Athens, Georgia 30602
© 2002 by the Southern Anthropological Society
All rights reserved
Set in 11/13 Times by Bookcomp, Inc.
Printed and bound by Maple-Vail
The paper in this book meets the guidelines for
permanence and durability of the Committee on
Production Guidelines for Book Longevity of the
Council on Library Resources.

Printed in the United States of America
06   05   04   03   02   C   5   4   3   2   1
06   05   04   03   02   P   5   4   3   2   1

Library of Congress Cataloging-in-Publication Data
Southern Indians and anthropologists : culture, politics, and identity /
edited by Lisa J. Lefler and Frederic W. Gleach.
p. cm. — (Southern Anthropological Society proceedings ; no. 35)
A collection of 11 papers from a symposium held
by the Society "at the turn of the millennium."
Includes bibliographical references.
ISBN 0-8203-2354-3 (alk. paper)
ISBN 0-8203-2355-1 (pbk. : alk. paper)
1. Indians of North America—Southern States—Research—Congresses.
2. Indians of North America—Study and teaching—Southern States—Congresses.
3. Anthropology—Southern States—Congresses.   I. Lefler, Lisa J.
II. Gleach, Frederic W. (Frederic Wright), 1960– III. Series.
GN2 .S9243 no. 35
[E78.S65]
301 s—dc21
[975.004'97]   2001043057

British Library Cataloging-in-Publication Data available

Contents

Southern Indians and
Anthropologists

Introduction

Lisa J. Lefler and Frederic W. Gleach

Much has already been written about the long and varied relationship between Indians and anthropologists, and about issues concerning Native communities (American Anthropological Association 1973; Biolsi and Zimmerman 1997; Champagne 1999; Mihesuah 1998; Paredes and Bonney 2001; Smith 1999; Thornton 1998; Warrior 1995). This volume is not intended to replace any of these other works, but rather to contribute to the discussion currently underway with examples of work now being done by anthropologists in various kinds of partnership with Indian communities in the U.S. South. The projects included reflect three of American anthropology's traditional subfields: anthropological linguistics, sociocultural anthropology, and archaeology. The communities to be discussed are the Yuchi of Oklahoma, the Chickasaw Nation of Oklahoma, the Eastern Band of Cherokee Indians in Western North Carolina, the Powhatans of Virginia, the Seminole Tribe of Florida, and the Waccamaw Siouan community of coastal North Carolina.

The communities and scholars were chosen to reflect contemporary as well as traditional senses of the southeastern United States (hereinafter referred to as the Southeast) and include certain groups that have sometimes been excluded from considerations of this geographic region. Inclusion of the Oklahoma tribes, for example, represents a reconfiguration of the region from Swanton's time, when the Southeast was a pristine area. At that time, Oklahoma was outside the area, although we now have an expanded view of Oklahoma's relation with the Southeast. Raymond Fogelson, the discussant at the symposium on which this volume is based, noted that the tribes of the Southeast have historically and politically been transnational, requiring a certain flexibility in defining boundaries. The Virginia Algonquians have sometimes been grouped with Algonquians of the northeastern U.S., although they are included in our discussion.

This symposium was constructed to discuss work *with*, rather than *about* American Indians of the Southeast. The papers by Jackson and Bender reflect such classic ethnographic methodologies as participant observation, formal and informal interviewing, and key-informant interviewing, demonstrating the rapport that is necessary for insight on gendered language use. Many of these papers also reflect the partnering of anthropologists and tribal members in projects such as language preservation and education, the study of fatherhood and related issues for policy and program development, the preservation of oral histories, archaeological research, and museum curation. Even those papers based on archival and historical research also rely on relationships with the people. As another of our discussants, Patricia Galloway, noted, these projects incorporate the work of anthropologists collaborating with Native people, where Native people are in control of the outcomes, to build culturally appropriate tools for universal problems that offer historically specific manifestations.

The work of these anthropologists illustrates the importance of understanding the influence of the past on the present, ethical reciprocity, the need to include Native voices, and the potential for continued partnered research. We recognize the honor and privilege of working with Indian communities, and also acknowledge the challenges that are presented to us. Linda Tuhiwai Smith (1999:10) poses these challenges as questions: "Whose research is it? Whose interests does it serve? Who will benefit from it? Who has designed its questions and framed its scope? Who will carry it out? Who will write it up? How will its results be disseminated?" And concerning the researcher, she asks, "Is her spirit clear? Does he have a good heart? What other baggage are they carrying? Are they useful to us? Can they fix up our generator? Can they actually do anything?" Such questions have been of real concern to the authors represented here.

Most anthropologists, Native and non-Native, agree that the time has come for a more humble and socially responsible approach to anthropological fieldwork. We believe that responsibility suggests trustworthiness, loyalty, reliability, and accountability—qualities that should characterize one's dedication and ethical obligation as a social scientist. When we partner with tribal nations, we enter an alliance and close association that directs our training and resources to issues that impact their communities. We live and work in the era of the Native American Graves Protection and Repatriation Act (NAGPRA), continuing challenges to Indian sovereignty, tribal bingo and casino gambling, tribal banking, and economic and cultural revitalization. We all, therefore, have had to reevaluate our attitudes and intentions, and check our academic egos at the door—specifically the tribal council door (Champagne 1999).

Tribal governments are rightly demanding that we be held accountable for our work by sharing our information and findings with the community. We may also be asked to assist in finding funding sources to initiate related programs; to help in developing tribal archives from our interviews; to make sure the words and voices of elders and other tribal members are an initial and integral part of the study design and a force in the direction of the research; to make collected oral histories available for future generations; to plan our study design and budgets to include gifts for our consultants, if appropriate; to make our work practical and/or reciprocal for the short and long term; and to assure communities that any royalties from publications will be left within the community. Those conducting clinical trials and medical research must be particularly careful to make their intentions and objectives clear through full disclosure and to take steps to make study findings easily accessible to the community.

No one would argue that the relationship between anthropologists and American Indians has ever been untroubled; questions have arisen since the inception of the discipline in the nineteenth century, and the same issues are evident in cultural relations that predate the founding of the discipline. What researchers focused on and looked for often told as much about them as it did about the people being studied. What can we learn from both the mistakes and the successes of anthropology's past that will make our current projects ethically sound and beneficial to the communities with whom we work? How can we turn fieldwork into a mutually enriching exchange?

This symposium took place at the turn of the millennium, perhaps an ideal time for reflection and evaluation, and it challenged us to discuss our future as well as our past. Walker's discussion of sacred texts reminds us to ask who owns those texts, and to consider our responsibilities regarding their representation. Discussants Karen Blu and Patricia Galloway point out that Gleach's research frames theoretical issues about how Indian identity may be constructed symbolically, while the papers by Duggan and Lerch show how that identity came to be played out performatively in terms of political activity and geographical movement. The work of Stans and Gopher illustrates how we can forge lasting partnerships based on service and reciprocity. Research by Lefler and Shannon points up the need for study that provides information to policy makers and tribal leaders engaged in the development of new programs; these papers also highlight the importance of identifying additional funding sources for the communities.

Discussant J. Anthony Paredes appropriately reminded the participants that anthropology is a comparative science and that our task is to find out as much as possible about humans around the world. We are working with people, and as such our work must be scientific, but certainly not without human feeling. Now is the time, therefore, for us to examine our approach and to ask: how do we do what we do? where will our work take us in the new millennium? how should we get there? what ways should we and our students take in order to build responsible partnerships? We eagerly look forward to new opportunities for service and collaboration.

We would like to take this opportunity to thank all our discussants— Karen Blu, Raymond D. Fogelson, Patricia Galloway, and J. Anthony Paredes—each of whom contributed extensively to the final versions of these papers. We were honored by their comments, insights, and overall conference participation.

REFERENCES

American Anthropological Association. 1973. *Anthropology and the American Indian: A Report of the Symposium on Anthropology and the American Indian*. San Francisco: The Indian Historian Press.

Biolsi, Thomas, and Larry J. Zimmerman, eds. 1997. *Indians and Anthropologists: Vine Deloria, Jr., and the Critique of Anthropology*. Tucson: University of Arizona Press.

Champagne, Duane, ed. 1999. *Contemporary Native American Cultural Issues*. Walnut Creek, Calif.: AltaMira.

Mihesuah, Devon A., ed. 1998. *Natives and Academics: Researching and Writing about American Indians*. Lincoln: University of Nebraska Press.

Paredes, J. Anthony, and Rachel Bonney, eds. 2001. *Anthropologists and Indians in the New South: A Retrospective for the New Millennium*. Tuscaloosa: University of Alabama Press.

Smith, Linda Tuhiwai. 1999. *Decolonizing Methodologies: Research and Indigenous Peoples*. New York: Zed Books.

Thornton, Russell, ed. 1998. *Studying Native America: Problems and Prospects*. Madison: University of Wisconsin Press.

Warrior, Robert Allen. 1995. *Tribal Secrets: Recovering American Indian Intellectual Traditions*. Minneapolis: University of Minnesota Press.

Powhatan Identity in Anthropology and Popular Culture (and Vice Versa)

Frederic W. Gleach

The Powhatans were the Native people who faced the first permanent English settlement in North America, and it is therefore only fitting that they be included in this examination of southeastern Indians in relation to anthropology.[1] I should note at the outset that my relation to the Powhatans has never been simply a professional choice, but developed from my personal history. I grew up in what was once Powhatan territory in central Virginia, and my family used to visit the Mattaponi and Pamunkey reservations when I was a child. I have clear memories of the annual photographs in the newspaper of Powhatan chiefs presenting deer and turkeys to the governor at Thanksgiving. I later did archaeological work that included Powhatan-related sites. I also conducted historical and archival research, revisited the reservations, and talked with Powhatan and other Native people at formal and informal gatherings of many sorts. Such long-term connections constitute a base for anthropological research, but in a more important way they also foster a personal sense of connectedness.

A number of anthropologists have written about the Powhatans (Feest 1990; Mooney 1890, 1907; Speck 1925, 1928), and I have contributed to that literature as well (Gleach 1992, 1997). The work of Rountree (1979, 1990, 1992) is particularly noteworthy with regard to their more recent history. As I sat down to write this paper, I began to wonder what more might possibly be said at this point; as Fogelson (1989:133) once wryly noted, having come up with a title, one finds oneself in the position of having to write a paper to justify it. I eventually realized that I had never really detailed some of the conceptual underpinnings of my recent work; this context might be an ideal place to do so.

I think it is important to define my terms precisely. The literature on ethnic identity is vast (e.g., Glazer and Moynihan 1975; Guibernau and Rex 1997; Sollors 1996; Wilmsen and McAllister 1996) and need not be reviewed here; but there are several relevant components of ethnic identity that can be teased from the concept, and for the sake of clarity I will use different labels for them. While these distinctions can be found in the literature they are seldom a major focus, although they are necessary for the specific issues at the heart of this paper.[2]

One aspect of identity is the internal meaning of the group: what does it mean to a member to be part of a group? How do "we" conceive of "ourselves," or how do "they" conceive of "themselves"? The answers to these questions constitute what I will refer to as *identity*—in this context, what sense do the Powhatans have of themselves? On the other hand, outsiders may (and often do) have a very different conception of the group and its meaning. When we ask how "we" conceive of "them" or how "they" conceive of "us," we are speaking of the group's *image*— in this paper, how do non-Powhatans think of the Powhatans?[3]

Representations are generated by both identity and image. A representation, in the specific sense intended here, is the manifestation in praxis of the cultural category. In linguistic and semiotic terms, a representation is a class of signs (Barthes 1968; Eco 1976; Hodge and Kress 1988; but see, by contrast, Brightman 1993:28–36; Eco 1986; Foucault 1973), but the more specific term seems appropriate here. As in the interpretation of photography (Tagg 1993), the term "representation" is intended to convey the complex web of relatedness and difference tying together the "original" as well as its literal representation, along with the act of interpretation involved in the interplay of the two (Barthes 1977; cf. Myers 1995). Representations of identity and image—not identities and images themselves, which are immaterial constructs—are received, interpreted, and responded to in cultural interaction, often employing what Sollors (1986:28) has called "contrastive strategies." The Powhatans represent themselves in various ways whenever they appear in public *as* Powhatans, including certain modes of dress, uses of language, and ritualized performances. Contexts for these representations include the previously mentioned annual presentation of turkey and deer to the governor, as well as public gatherings or powwows, and even world fairs and other expositions. Others also construct representations of the Powhatans, most visibly in recent years through the Disney film *Pocahontas*, but also in plays, works of art, and written accounts, including historical and anthropological texts.

Representations may be seen as doing the work of identity. They are often consciously deployed to effect a particular end. They are explicitly political statements, declaring their intent to all who can read them. Reading, however, is never perfect: representations are cultural signs, and just as a written text can be given divergent readings, so the meaning intended to be communicated by a particular representation may not be the one actually received by the audience. Processes akin to the traditional practices of deconstructing arguments must be employed in analyzing representations. Using techniques of deconstruction here does not, however, mean following the current vogue of making the process of deconstruction itself (and the scholar undertaking it) the focus of interest; in fact, this context highlights the problems with that approach. My take as a scholar on an act of representation has little or no effect on the ways that representation may be read and responded to by real participants in cultural interactions. But the process of representation, reading, and response does have very real implications and consequences. These themes and techniques have been appropriated by some as new and postmodern, but they actually have roots in several scholarly traditions, particularly interpretive anthropology (e.g., Geertz 1963).

Identity, image, and representation rely on the processes of *boundary definition* and *boundary maintenance*. Who is in the group, and who is not—and how is such membership determined? These are very serious issues that have received considerable scholarly attention (e.g., F. Barth 1969). Individuals' lives are directly affected by these definitions. But political aspects of identity are not confined to these questions; rather, they include the subtler effects of meaning, such as positive and negative valuations in various degrees, and shadings of interpersonal and intergroup relationships, forming a kind of semiotics of identity.

Image seems potentially much more complex than identity. Whereas identity is determined by a group that self-defines as coherent, images of that group are held by people of diverse backgrounds and need not be all the same. There can be significant individual variations in the images of a single group. But I am interested in painting with broad strokes, emphasizing the general cultural frameworks of identity interactions. Such an analysis must be drawn from the specifics of individual practice, however, as instantiations of meaning, which are themselves readings and thus inherently cultural, political, and subjective. No claim of objectivity can or should be inferred in any social analysis, then; one thinks of Ricoeur's (1965) distinction between good and bad subjectivities.

There is nonetheless an important context in which claims of conventional objectivity do take place: courtroom testimony. Driven by necessity, Native Americans are increasingly turning to the courts to define and affirm their identity. Court decisions do establish these definitions as objective fact in the legal context (although social use can and does often still diverge). Indeed, the legal system itself explicitly demands that evidentiary testimony also be cast as objective, which means that anthropological testimony that recognizes the social, constructed nature of "facts" has been dismissed in some cases (Campisi 1991). We must work to educate nonspecialists concerning such distinctions. At a conference in Cuba in 1997, I was party to a discussion of anthropology and its applications that highlighted these issues; the relevance and utility of research is a major concern in Cuba, and is increasingly so for those of us working in the United States and elsewhere. *Participatory action research* or *action science* (Argyris, Putnam, and Smith 1985), terms encompassing contemporary approaches that direct theoretically and methodologically sound research toward a practical application in a way reminiscent of Tax's *action anthropology* (Gearing 1970; Gearing, Netting, and Peattie 1960; Tax 1958) or the Cornell Peru Project at Vicos (Dobyns, Doughty, and Lasswell 1971; Holmberg 1966), assume a critical importance in this context.

As a humanistic anthropologist, I believe that the essential first step in working toward our goals of responsibility and partnership is consideration of the consequences of our constructions, based in personal relationships with the people we write about. We did not need anyone to tell us that objectivity is an unobtainable goal; the valuable insights from individual perspectives and relationships have long been recognized in anthropology and elsewhere. Since our images of the Powhatans are shaped by and expressed through representations, it is crucial to examine these representations, and perhaps attempt to produce new ones with different meanings and/or different articulations with identity and image, in order to bring about positive changes in understandings. Since we recognize that all our interpretations, understandings, analyses, and representations are social constructs a step removed from the underlying constructs of identity and image, it may be possible to revise our modern images of the Powhatans to better reflect the images, and even the identities, of the past. We can never represent "truth," but we can at least attempt to make our representations more faithful to reality. In recasting the history of seventeenth-century relations between the Powhatans and the colonists, for example, I sought to demonstrate (Gleach 1997) the ways Powhatan and English identities, English images of the Powhatans, and Powhatan images of the English all articulated (through representation) in historical processes to produce both the stories we know and the consequences of those stories. My hope was to foster better understanding, and thus ultimately some improvement in the social position and lives of the Powhatan people. It may not be the most direct form of social action, but since it deals with the fundamental issues of identity and history, it seems to me to have the greatest potential.

My more recent work on the Powhatans has revolved around issues of representation and the political consequences thereof in the twentieth century. One project explores the representation of our images of Pocahontas; another examines both images and identity of the Powhatans through their representations at the 1907 Jamestown Tercentennial Exposition. I am currently preparing a study of Speck's work with the Powhatans from the 1920s through the 1940s, focusing on his representations of the Powhatans, their connections to his own identity, and the ways they were intended for and used by the Powhatans themselves. The first two projects therefore focus on representations in the realm of popular culture, while the third deals with representations in the anthropological literature.

The story of Pocahontas is undoubtedly the best-known representation of the Powhatan Indians. From Captain Smith's own writings to the Disney film, non-Powhatans have appropriated this story for various purposes. Green (1975) was the first scholar to explore these representations, a project carried on by Tilton (1994), among others. In the early nineteenth century, as American national identity began to form and the eastern Indians were increasingly marginalized both literally and metaphorically, Pocahontas became an icon of an idealized, naturalized (and fictional) past, serving as a model of the ideals of duty and self-sacrifice, and as an example of the possibilities of bringing Christian conversion and civilization to the Indians. Her story was also taken up by southerners interested in reclaiming priority in the founding of the U.S. in opposition to New England–based historians, who emphasized the Pilgrims and Plymouth in their national foundation myths. From that time the Pocahontas story took on a life of its own, and numerous different versions were produced over the years. Children's books, epic poems, the literary novel *The Sotweed Factor* (J. Barth 1960), a popular romance novel (Donnell 1991), dolls, advertisements, plays, and movies have all been derived from the story. At present the most prominent Pocahontas production remains the 1995 Disney film, which hijacks the historical actors for the sake of heavy-handed multicultural propaganda.[4] These representations were all produced by non-Powhatans for consumption by other non-Powhatans, and most have little to offer in terms of understanding the real Powhatan Indians. They do, however, reflect our images of the Powhatans and of Native Americans in general: sometimes savage, sometimes romanticized, sometimes feminized, but generally "close to nature." Most important, perhaps, they are depicted as subject to our demands. We represent them as we see fit at any given time.

Dramatic representations of the Pocahontas story have been presented since at least the beginning of the nineteenth century (Custis 1803), but the story was also performed for a number of years by the Powhatans themselves, for their own purposes. I believe Feest (1990) was the first scholar to pay attention to these performances. In terms of the framework presented here, the Powhatans devised a public representation of their identity to counter the images non-Powhatans had constructed of them. These public performances were staged many times in the late nineteenth and early twentieth centuries, but perhaps the most noteworthy context was the Jamestown Tercentennial Exposition, which brought together representations by the Powhatans of their own identity and representations of the non-Powhatan image.

Organizers of the Jamestown Exposition intended to commemorate the founding of the town, but they had other goals in mind as well. They wanted to showcase Virginia, and by extension the South, on the national and international stage, demonstrating that forty years of Reconstruction had brought modern qualities to the region without destroying its historical heritage. They also wanted to celebrate the military (especially naval) power of the United States, which had been demonstrated by the quick defeat of Spain in the 1898 war. It was similarly important to demonstrate the ways the former Spanish colonies were being improved under U.S. rule. Given these strongly patriotic themes (most of which derive from events that occurred long after the titular founding of

Jamestown), it is perhaps not surprising that the Powhatans and the events of 1607 were largely relegated to secondary status. The most striking presence of Native people at the Exposition was in the Wild West Show, put on by the 101 Ranch of Oklahoma and featuring mostly Indians of the Plains. The amusements area at the Exposition was called the Warpath, and representations of Native Americans were used there, as elsewhere at the Exposition, that depicted generic Indians in Plains regalia. The intended message of these images was clear: Indians were creatures of the West, and of the past.

Although their presence was noted in only one published record I have found (Slosson 1907), the Powhatans did in fact participate in the Jamestown Exposition: a group of Pamunkeys performed their dramatic reenactment of the rescue of Captain John Smith by Pocahontas. A pair of stereoscopic photographs taken at the exposition document that performance. The costumes were those typically worn by Powhatans for traditional/formal public events circa 1907, with turkey-feather collars and headdresses and a mix of buckskin and textiles. According to Slosson (1907:125), "A band of these Pamaunkees on the Warpath—the modern, peaceful Warpath—nightly re-enact the historic and legendary deeds of their ancestors. As they have not had the advantage of college training, their war whoops are deficient in animation and abandon, but they have brought with them from their reservation the genuine original stone on which Captain Smith did or did not lay his head when he was or was not rescued by Pocahontas." Slosson was generally critical of the Jamestown Exposition, as were many of the northern commentators, who referred to it as the "Jamestown Imposition." But even a more sympathetic observer would have been hard pressed to take the Pamunkeys seriously, located as they were on the Warpath for their performance. The Pamunkeys were attempting to use this stage to increase public awareness of their continued existence, just as Virginia was trying to use it to demonstrate progress, but the message was not generally received as intended. To the extent that the Powhatans were seen at all, they were mostly just entertaining icons from the past.

Several other instances of Powhatans offering representations of their identity to the public warrant at least brief consideration. I have already mentioned the annual presentations to the governor, which are regularly covered in the news. The chiefs making the presentation also "dress Indian" to help mark their identity, although today the attire is usually

Plains-style buckskins and feather bonnets, a mode demanded by the popular conception of how Indians dress. Eastern traditions are not read in the desired way by non-Native people. A style of pottery making, developed in the 1930s in consultation with an art teacher, was also intended to look more Indian (Stern 1951:59–66), and today some potters are returning to materials and techniques more reminiscent of prehistoric Powhatan pottery. There are also now social powwows, a kind of performance seen by the non-Native public as authentically Indian. Through the twentieth century, the Powhatans developed and revised representations of their Native identity that could be perceived properly by the non-Native public. While these processes are dismissed by some as "invented traditions," it is essential to remember that all cultural traditions are invented, and dynamic. We should no more expect Native people today to dress in animal-hide loincloths and live in bark-covered houses than we expect descendants of the First Families of Virginia to dress in seventeenth-century English attire, live in one-room post-in-ground houses, and be ignorant of the use of the table fork. While their public representations have increasingly drawn on pan-Indian markers, the Powhatans have retained their specific identity. Through the Pocahontas story, their continuity in central Virginia and their relationship to the land reinforces their internal discourse (Rountree 1990:187–218, 243–68; 1992; but see Fogelson 1998 for a contrasting view).

A less familiar example of Powhatan representation dates to the mid-nineteenth century. In 1844 a free black named Armstrong Archer published an antislavery tract in London. Archer's mother was a Powhatan Indian, and he had grown up in that community. By the late nineteenth century the Powhatans were trying to mark themselves off from African Americans, but in the first two centuries after Jamestown they had been open to others, including African Americans, who chose to live with them, intermarry, and, in some cases, adopt Powhatan culture. A person's appearance was less important than his or her cultural behavior. This principle would have resonated within the antislavery movement, and it was in this context that Archer told his story. He recounted his family history and included a story from the seventeenth century that he learned as a child among the Powhatans (Gleach 1992). Archer almost certainly did not intend to shape perceptions of the Powhatans in the general population, but his tract demonstrates how Powhatan identity may be deployed for different ends.

Anthropologists have sometimes been employed by the Powhatans as part of the struggle to maintain their identity. In the 1890s they were visited by the Smithsonian anthropologists Albert Gatschet (n.d.) and James Mooney (1907). Although Gatschet's notebook was never formally published, Mooney did publish a piece to help commemorate the 300th anniversary of the settlement at Jamestown. In that article he noted an 1887 Pamunkey law prohibiting marriage with blacks. Racial tensions were near a peak, with legislators attempting to define anyone with "one drop" of non-white blood into a generic "Colored" category. This "one drop rule" was codified in 1924 as the Virginia Racial Integrity Law, and state officials fervently pursued its application to the Powhatans and other Virginia Indians (Rountree 1990:219–37). The only exception allowed was for those whose only non-Caucasian ancestry was one-sixteenth or less American Indian, a loophole designed to accommodate those prominent whites who were proudly descended from Pocahontas. There is no evidence that the Powhatans had any desire to pass as white, which is what those who produced the Racial Integrity Law feared most. Their efforts to preserve their distinctive communities attest to their desire to keep their own identity. Mooney had noted that the Powhatans continued to "pride themselves upon their descent from the warriors of Powhatan" (1890:132). Nevertheless, application of the Racial Integrity Law meant that Powhatans serving in the military or going to schools, prisons, or other institutions were placed in "colored" facilities, which were generally inferior to their white counterparts. The Powhatans, who for centuries had been receptive to outsiders regardless of race, were thus forced by the racialized situation of the time to recognize and institute the racial categories of mainstream America.

The anthropologist most closely associated with the Powhatans, Frank Speck, first visited them in 1914. He made other visits from 1919 through the 1920s; beginning in 1939 he returned with groups of students. The publications that resulted from his work seem to have been designed to give the tribes information and scholarly backing in their fight against racism. As a result, state officials tried to have Speck's books banned from public libraries in Virginia. Speck wrote about Powhatan history and culture change, but he also touched on those aspects of the traditional culture that were still to be found. No observer could miss the cultural changes that had taken place; Speck, however, emphasized the more easily overlooked continuities.

Speck had been trained by Franz Boas and shared with him and many of his students a deep concern over the racial policies of the time. But unlike Boas and some of his followers, Speck did not work directly to oppose such policies. Speck himself claimed mixed blood; he was part Mahican and had been raised as a child by the last native speaker of Pequot. He was more comfortable in the company of Indians than in the academic circles in which much of his life was spent (Blankenship 1991). Had he directly contested racist policies, he could easily have been dismissed as self-serving. So in good Native fashion he took an indirect approach, providing the tools for people to fight their own fight, and subverting racist policies in his everyday life.

After the United States entered the Second World War, the Powhatans faced a new challenge. Powhatan inductees in the 1940s were classified as "Negro" (not the case for those who had served in the First World War) based on their birth certificates, which had been altered after the passage of the Racial Integrity Law. At least one individual was imprisoned for refusing such classification, prompting renewed intensity in Speck's investigative research. Preserved in his papers are many letters from this period, along with a copy of a Virginia Selective Service office memorandum ("Procedure for Classification of Persons Registered as Indians"). The individual who protested was paroled after about a month, but the correspondence continued beyond the end of the war (Speck died in 1950).

By retelling some stories of the interactions of anthropology, popular culture, and the Powhatan Indians, I hope to elucidate the ways ethnic and racial categories have been deployed, by the Powhatans as well as by others, and the goals and effects of those actions. If we can come to understand these processes, we should be able to act and create more responsibly in our lives and in our work. The distinction maintained here between identity and image, and the recognition of representation as a process that pertains to both, are intended to clarify these processes. The subtleties of meaning in the context of ethnic identities require analysis that is sensitive to and informed by the specific situation, explicitly recognizing the political relations involved. The ideal situation may be collaborative research, although such projects cannot entirely shield the researcher from controversy. Even non-collaborative research needs to be based on an understanding that our research concerns people and situations that have political connotations. The partnerships of anthropologists and the people we study are present whether we recognize them or not, simply by the nature of our work, and we thus have an inescapable responsibility to those people.

NOTES

1. I am grateful to Lisa Lefler for inviting me to participate in this symposium and thus forcing me to think through my understandings of identity. Karen Blu, Raymond Fogelson, Patricia Galloway, and members of the audience in Mobile offered thoughtful comments, and I have tried to incorporate many of their suggestions here. A course I taught in fall 1999, "Cultural Diversity and Contemporary Issues," also dealt with some of these issues, and conversations with my teaching assistants, Thamora Fishel, Alexander Newell, and Irene Limpe, helped me to organize my thoughts on this complex topic.

2. There are many ways to approach and categorize processes of identity. Fogelson (1998) draws somewhat different distinctions, based on earlier work with psychological models (Wallace and Fogelson 1965), but his framework is generally compatible with mine.

3. Comaroff's "*attribution* of collective identity . . . on the part of others" (1987:53) evokes the process, but the semiotic specifics and parallels between identity and image are not his focus. Both are dynamic and diachronic constructive processes, and are often interrelated, as discussed below in the Powhatan case.

4. See Strong (1996) for a more appreciative view of Disney's *Pocahontas*.

REFERENCES

Archer, Armstrong. 1844. *A Compendium of Slavery, As It Exists in the Present Day U.S. of A*. London: J. Haddon.

Argyris, Chris, Robert Putnam, and Diana McLain Smith. 1985. *Action Science: Concepts, Methods, and Skills for Research and Intervention*. San Francisco: Jossey-Bass.

Barth, Fredrik. 1969. Introduction to *Ethnic Groups and Boundaries: The Social Organization of Cultural Difference*, ed. Fredrik Barth. 9–38. Boston: Little, Brown.

Barth, John. 1960. *The Sotweed Factor*. Garden City, N.Y.: Doubleday.

Barthes, Roland. 1968. *Elements of Semiology*, trans. Annette Lavers and Colin Smith. New York: Hill and Wang.

————. 1977. *Image, Music, Text*, trans. Stephen Heath. New York: Hill and Wang.

Blankenship, Roy, ed. 1991. *The Life and Times of Frank G. Speck, 1881–1950*. Philadelphia: Department of Anthropology, University of Pennsylvania.

Brightman, Robert. 1993. *Grateful Prey: Rock Cree Human-Animal Relationships*. Berkeley: University of California Press.

Campisi, Jack. 1991. *The Mashpee Indians: Tribe on Trial*. Syracuse, N.Y.: Syracuse University Press.

Comaroff, John. 1987. Of Totemism and Ethnicity. In *Ethnography and the Historical Imagination*, ed. John Comaroff and Jean Comaroff. 26–50. Boulder, Colo.: Westview.

Custis, George Washington Parke. 1803. *Pocahontas, or the Settlers of Virginia, a National Drama in Three Acts*. Philadelphia: C. Alexander.

Dobyns, Henry F., Paul L. Doughty, and Harold D. Lasswell, eds. 1971. *Peasants, Power, and Applied Social Change: Vicos as a Model*. Beverly Hills, Calif.: Sage.

Donnell, Susan. 1991. *Pocahontas*. New York: Berkley Books.

Eco, Umberto. 1976. *A Theory of Semiotics*. Bloomington: Indiana University Press.

————. 1986. *Travels in Hyperreality: Essays*, trans. William Weaver. New York: Harcourt Brace Jovanovich.

Feest, Christian. 1990. Pride and Prejudice: The Pocahontas Myth and the Pamunkey. In *The Invented Indian: Cultural Fictions and Government Policies*, ed. James A. Clifton. 87–104. New Brunswick, N.J.: Transaction.

Fogelson, Raymond D. 1989. The Ethnohistory of Events and Nonevents. *Ethnohistory* 36(2):133–47.

————. 1998. Perspectives on Native American Identity. In *Studying Native America: Problems and Prospects*, ed. Russell Thornton. 50–73. Madison: University of Wisconsin Press.

Foucault, Michel. 1973. *The Order of Things: An Archaeology of the Human Sciences*. New York: Vintage Books.

Gatschet, Albert S. n.d. *Pamunkey Notebook*. Washington, D.C.: National Anthropological Archives, Ms. 2197.

Gearing, Frederick O. 1970. *The Face of the Fox*. Chicago: Aldine.

Gearing, Frederick O., Robert McC. Netting, and Lisa R. Peattie, eds. 1960. *Documentary History of the Fox Project, 1948–1959: A Program in Action Anthropology, Directed by Sol Tax*. Chicago: Department of Anthropology, University of Chicago.

Geertz, Clifford. 1963. *The Interpretation of Culture*. New York: Basic Books.

Glazer, Nathan, and Daniel P. Moynihan, eds. 1975. *Ethnicity: Theory and Experience*. Cambridge, Mass.: Harvard University Press.

Gleach, Frederic W. 1992. A Traditional Story of the Powhatan Indians Recorded in the Early Nineteenth Century. In *Papers of the Twenty-third Algonquian Conference*, ed. William Cowan. 40–48. Ottawa: Carleton University.

———. 1997. *Powhatan's World and Colonial Virginia: A Conflict of Cultures*. Lincoln: University of Nebraska Press.

Green, Rayna. 1975. The Pocahontas Perplex: The Image of Indian Women in American Culture. *Massachusetts Review* 16(4):698–714.

Guibernau, Montserrat, and John Rex, eds. 1997. *The Ethnicity Reader: Nationalism, Multiculturalism and Migration*. Cambridge, U.K.: Polity Press.

Hodge, Robert, and Gunther Kress. 1988. *Social Semiotics*. Ithaca, N.Y.: Cornell University Press.

Holmberg, Allen R. 1966. *Vicos: Método y Prática de Antropología Aplicada*. Lima, Peru: Editorial Estudios Andinos.

Mooney, James. 1890. The Powhatan Indians. *American Anthropologist* 3:132.

———. 1907. The Powhatan Confederacy, Past and Present. *American Anthropologist*, n.s. 9(1):129–52.

Myers, Fred R. 1995. Representing Culture: The Production of Discourse(s) for Aboriginal Acrylic Paintings. In *The Traffic in Culture: Refiguring Art and Anthropology*, ed. George E. Marcus and Fred R. Myers. 37–49. Berkeley: University of California Press.

Ricoeur, Paul. 1965. Objectivity and Subjectivity in History. In *History and Truth*, ed. Paul Ricoeur, trans. Charles A. Kelbley. 1–31. Evanston, Ill.: Northwestern University Press.

Rountree, Helen C. 1979. The Indians of Virginia: A Third Race in a Biracial State. In *Southeastern Indians Since the Removal Era*, ed. Walter L. Williams. 105–118. Athens: University of Georgia Press.

———. 1990. *Pocahontas's People: The Powhatan Indians of Virginia through Four Centuries*. Norman: University of Oklahoma Press.

———. 1992. Indian Virginians on the Move. In *Indians of the Southeastern United States in the Late 20th Century*, ed. J. Anthony Paredes. 96–112. Tuscaloosa: University of Alabama Press.

Slosson, Edwin E. 1907. Round about Jamestown. *The Independent* 63 (July 18):123–9.

Sollors, Werner. 1986. *Beyond Ethnicity: Consent and Descent in American Culture*. New York: Oxford University Press.

———, ed. 1996. *Theories of Ethnicity: A Classical Reader*. New York: New York University Press.

Speck, Frank G. 1925. *The Rappahannock Indians of Virginia*. New York: Heye Foundation.

———. 1928. *Chapters on the Ethnology of the Powhatan Tribes of Virginia*. New York: Heye Foundation.

Stern, Theodore. 1951. *Pamunkey Pottery Making*. Chapel Hill: Archaeological Society of North Carolina.

Strong, Pauline Turner. 1996. Animated Indians: Critique and Contradiction in a Commodified Children's Culture. *Cultural Anthropology* 11(3):405–24.

Tagg, John. 1993. *The Burden of Representation: Essays on Photographies and Histories*. Minneapolis: University of Minnesota Press.

Tax, Sol. 1958. The Fox Project. *Human Organization* 17:17–19.

Tilton, Robert S. 1994. *Pocahontas: The Evolution of an American Narrative*. Cambridge: Cambridge University Press.

Wallace, Anthony F. C., and Raymond D. Fogelson. 1965. The Identity Struggle. In *Intensive Family Therapy: Theoretical and Practical Aspects*, ed. Ivan Boszomenyi-Nagy and James L. Framo. 44–60. New York: Harper and Row.

Wilmsen, Edwin N., and Patrick McAllister, eds. 1996. *The Politics of Difference: Ethnic Premises in a World of Power*. Chicago: University of Chicago Press.

In the Service of Native Interests: Archaeology for, of, and by Cherokee People

Brett Riggs

During the past decade, members of the Eastern Band of Cherokee Indians have increasingly voiced interest in and concern about archaeological resource management issues. Tribal policies toward and management of such resources have gradually evolved from reactive, incident-specific responses into a formally organized program under the newly constituted Tribal Historic Preservation Office. This paper presents a personal perspective on a series of key events that have driven the development of current tribal policy. During these episodes, relations between archaeologists and the native community have ranged from open confrontation to active partnership. Lessons from these encounters have not been cumulative, although the native and archaeological communities are gradually building rules of engagement that accommodate the interests of both groups in the conservation of archaeological resources.

My personal experience with archaeology and the Eastern Band of Cherokee Indians began in 1990, when I approached the tribal council with an abstract of my dissertation proposal for research on nineteenth-century Cherokee ethnohistory and archaeology. I had intended this to be a *pro forma* courtesy notice of work that did not involve tribal lands or living tribal members, and I hoped and anticipated that my proposed work would be of interest and use to some Eastern Band members. I knew several members of the council, and my abstract came to the floor under the sponsorship of a tribal member. I naively thought that my proposed work would be summarily noted in council, and I would be dismissed, perhaps with some word of thanks for recognizing the Cherokees' interest in their heritage. After I gave a brief synopsis of my project, I nervously waited for comment under the glare of the live camera that broadcast to the reservation's closed circuit. The council chairman arose, fixed me with a fierce gaze, then unleashed an articulate, scathing tirade on the endless stream of researchers who plundered the Cherokees for dissertation data, then gave nothing in return. Particularly noxious were the archaeologists, who went about digging into the graves of Cherokee ancestors to plunder their last belongings as a final act of conquest. He concluded with a challenge for me to justify my proposed work and my profession.

Although taken aback, I hastily attempted to frame my research in terms of educational benefits to the tribe, and I defended the humanistic value of work on family farmsteads that living Cherokees could embrace as their ancestral homes. The council then began its debate; half the members voiced opinions on the value of archaeology (or lack thereof) and the validity of my work. When questioned about native graves, I responded that I did not expect to find any, and swore that I would not excavate any graves that I might encounter. I just wanted to dig around in people's trash heaps. One councilwoman declared, "Well, maybe I don't want anybody going through my grandmama's trash."

In the end, the council concluded that I was probably harmless, admonished me to keep the tribe informed of my progress, then passed a resolution approving my research. Outside the council chambers and away from the all-seeing camera, several council members approached me, shook my hand, and expressed personal interest in my proposed work. Some of the more vehement critics on the council even smiled, nodded, and exchanged pleasantries. One member informed me that the inquisition was largely a matter of political posturing for the tribal audience that watched council sessions on the tribal channel. When I stopped at the reservation McDonald's for coffee, the server, a Cherokee woman with *Tsa-la-gi* tattooed in Sequoyan syllabary on her forearm, exclaimed, "Hey, I just saw you on TV! You know, they shouldn't have treated you that way."

I left Qualla Boundary thoroughly chastened and somewhat bewildered, yet I resolved to pursue my own project in ways that would directly benefit tribal heritage interests. It was clear that Cherokee perceptions of archaeology ran a wide gamut, but the dominant feeling was that archaeology was something that white people did to native people, rather than being a pursuit for and by Indians. For many Cherokees, archaeology is just another repressive political act by Anglo-American society; the prevalence of this feeling renders archaeology a useful topic for internal debate. My presentation before the council supplied a convenient and safe issue over which rivals in tribal government could spar.

As it turned out, I had unwittingly walked into the middle of council deliberations on a much more serious archaeological subject. During the late spring of 1990, U.S. Forest Service law enforcement officers arrested several vandals in the act of looting native burials from Lake Hole Cave on federal lands in northeastern Tennessee. Federal prosecutors seized the opportunity to build a case for a precedent-setting conviction with real penalties. The Forest Service archaeologist for Tennessee approached the Eastern Band tribal council, informed them of the potential significance of the case, and asked for the support of the tribe in the government's case. After months of investigation and a dramatic trial, which included tribal members' testimony on the importance and sacredness of native graves, federal prosecutors secured six convictions on various charges. Most of the tribal council, as well as other tribal members, attended the sentencing phase of the trial; their presence and comments influenced the judge to impose stiff fines and actual prison times on the grave desecrators.

Among the physical evidence used in the trial were the human bones exhumed by the vandals. Following the trial, the Forest Service, in keeping with its own burial policy (this being prior to the implementation of the federal Native American Graves Protection and Repatriation Act, or NAGPRA), repatriated the remains to the Eastern Band, and tribal authorities turned the remains over to a traditional religious organization for reburial.

The Lake Hole Cave case influenced the development of tribal policy and attitudes in a number of ways. First, the case led to a formalization of the processes of archaeological consultation and official tribal participation in archaeological resource issues. Second, since the case was reported in the tribal press, there was heightened tribal awareness about archaeological resource issues and an increase in the understanding of tribal members about archaeological resource legislation. Third, the case placed the tribe in an advocacy role in a successful federal case; this situation defined the Eastern Band as key players in cultural resource management issues in the region. Fourth, the case fixed the concept of repatriation and reburial in the Eastern Band. Such procedures had been introduced with the earlier reburial of Overhill Cherokee remains on tribal lands at Vonore, Tennessee, but the reburial of the Lake Hole Cave remains was the first such instance on Qualla Boundary. Fifth, archaeological efforts at stabilization and restoration of the vandalized cave deposits involved Cherokee students as appointed monitors and participants, thus beginning a trend of Cherokee student participation in archaeological excavations at the Chattooga, Cullowhee Valley, Brasstown Valley, and Warren Wilson sites.

All these developments appear to have had a positive effect on tribal perceptions of archaeology (if not of archaeologists), and a new phase of tribal participation and partnership in archaeological resource management was inaugurated. With the passage and eventual implementation of NAGPRA, Eastern Band representatives began touring repositories that held collections of human remains and artifacts from the traditional Cherokee homelands; they reported back to the council as they determined which archaeologists and institutions were naughty and which were nice.

The tribe expanded its control and official interest in archaeological issues in 1993, when the Museum of the Cherokee Indian secured a National Park Service grant for an archaeological survey of select tracts on Qualla Boundary. This was the first archaeological project that the tribe actually initiated and actively guided. Although the project was directed by outside archaeologists, myself included, the team included Eastern Band members who mediated most community encounters to the extent that the project came to be widely regarded as a tribal endeavor. We *unega* (literally "white," but with a pejorative connotation) archaeologists were perceived as working for the tribe, and most tribal members indulgently tolerated our presence. One elderly Cherokee gentleman who visited the crew even informed us that he had worked on WPA excavations and had wanted to become an archaeologist, but economic circumstances did not permit him to pursue his ambitions. Only one tribal member voiced open antipathy toward our work; this university-educated individual had been involved in repatriation in the West, and had recently returned to Cherokee territory.

Despite the tribe's ever-increasing involvement in archaeological and repatriation consultation and other archaeological resource management issues, the Eastern Band still had no central clearinghouse for handling such affairs, nor were there any formal guidelines or written policy to provide case-to-case consistency. Management was largely event-driven and dependent on personal interactions; emergent policy was ad hoc and case-specific. Toward the end of 1994, the tribal administration entered into a period of disarray, with allegations of embezzlement and other malfeasance leading to official investigations and eventually to the impeachment of the chief. In this environment, such petty matters as inquiries for archaeological consultation with the tribe were either ignored or handed off to committee members for desultory attention. The climate of governmental disorder within the Eastern Band, coupled with the continued lack of formal policy and procedures for consultation, contributed to a highly publicized dispute over archaeological salvage and grave removal in the tribe's own backyard. In 1995, Macon County, North Carolina, began development of an industrial site that was known from previous investigations to contain native graves. In the absence of clear-cut federal involvement in the project, the only apparent protection accorded to the site was the North Carolina burial statute, which required that the graves should be relocated prior to construction. The county commission contacted the North Carolina Office of State Archaeology, which aided the county in soliciting bids for archaeological salvage and burial removal. The state office also initiated consultation with Eastern Band representatives, and achieved a verbal (but not written) agreement condoning the work. When the archaeological fieldwork commenced at the industrial site in August 1995, the scale of the project excited the attention of local activists, who began to agitate for cessation of burial removal. These activists organized public meetings, rallies, marches, and prayer vigils to protest the development of the industrial park and the excavation of native graves. They also enlisted support from the traditional Cherokee religious organization that had managed the reinterring of the Lake Hole Cave remains; members of this organization mobilized tribal sentiment against the burial salvage. Bumper stickers reading, "I don't shop in Macon County—it's a *grave* decision" began appearing on Indian vehicles around the reservation.

As controversy over the Macon County project heated up, landmark tribal elections unseated the old governing dynasty, replacing half of the council and installing a new, reform-minded chief, Joyce Duggan. During the televised council session, the new government heard tribal members passionately condemn the burial salvage as desecration. Sensing the weight of tribal sentiment against the Macon County project, the chief and council reversed the earlier administration's opinion (which was never signed or ratified) and officially denounced the continued removal of native graves from the industrial park, while cautiously supporting other aspects of the archaeological work. This pronouncement, together with highly publicized protests in Macon County, drove Caterpillar, Inc., the prospective client for the industrial site, to abandon the project.

The Macon County board of commissioners was livid over the loss of anticipated employment and industrial revenues, and forged ahead to eliminate the encumbrances to its property. At that point, the North Carolina Archaeological Society, together with the Eastern Band and a number of local interest groups, began a drive to raise money to purchase the site for preservation. This effort, led by the state's regional archaeologist, amassed funds to acquire the property, but the county called off the deal when protesters riled the commissioners with continued civil disobedience. The county finally agreed to abandon its development plans, cap the site with fill dirt, and use the location for a drivers' training course.

The Macon County incident left a bitter aftertaste. The county commission resented the intrusion of the Eastern Band, and some commissioners felt that the archaeologists were in league with the tribe and local protest groups. The plan for use of the site in drivers' training was acceptable to the Eastern Band, but offended local activists, who felt the site should be preserved as green space. For many Eastern Band members, the episode cast archaeology (and its practitioners) in a very negative light as the evil twin of commercial development.

For the new chief and council of the Easter Band, the industrial site episode dramatically illustrated the pressing need to address cultural resource issues in a coherent and cohesive manner. This attitude was reinforced by a concurrent project on tribal lands. Pursuant to a casino gaming compact involving the tribe, the National Indian Gaming Commission (NIGC), and the state of North Carolina, the Eastern Band began development of a major casino complex at a site along Soco Creek on Qualla Boundary. Planning for the casino, which was supervised by the NIGC, required compliance with the National Historic Preservation Act, including inventory and assessment of archaeological resources in the project area. Our 1993 survey of this locality identified an archaeologi-

cal site with buried deposits that extended beneath a six-acre paved parking lot; the NIGC and the state's historic protection office requested definition of the total extent, content, and integrity of the site prior to further development. Archaeological contractors (myself included)
removed the parking lot and excavated test trenches through compact
fill dirt, exposing a portion of a fifteenth-century Cherokee hamlet with
at least six houses and associated hearths and pits. Site testing also
revealed a single grave, located at the center of the proposed casino. This
discovery touched off a planning crisis; in order for the casino development to proceed in this location, the grave (and probably a dozen more)
would have to be moved, although the tribe had just issued a public
proclamation denouncing the removal of graves for commercial development. The chief quickly decided that the tribe and casino could not
afford the public relations backlash from a policy double standard, and
decreed that the casino should be moved to a different location, thereby
sacrificing almost $200,000 in groundwork, planning, and design. When
the casino was built nearby, the hamlet site was covered with fill dirt and
repaved for casino parking; a lone memorial and small green space
marks the single identified grave. Chief Duggan was lauded for her decision to apply the same policy of burial preservation to a tribal development project as to a nontribal industrial park. Many tribal members,
however, questioned the appropriateness of "preserving" graves beneath
a parking lot, and some of them regard the casino and parking lot as
haunted.

In the Macon County fiasco, archaeologists were vilified; by contrast,
archaeologists involved with the casino site project were generally perceived as preservationists working in the interest of the tribe. We were
informed that we were considered just the finders, not the destroyers of
the grave, and we were praised for being honest enough to tell people
what was at the site. Had we been directed to excavate the site and
remove burials for the casino construction, we would certainly have
been labeled desecrators and grave looters. Instead, the casino project
came to be regarded by many tribal members as a model for tribal
responsibility and control in archaeology. Tolerance and acceptance of
archaeology by the tribe are clearly context-specific.

While the Macon County and casino site projects were in process, Chief
Duggan appointed Lynn Harlan to organize a Cultural Resources Division
within the tribal government, in part to coordinate archaeological resource

issues for the tribe. Harlan, a university-educated tribal member who had dealt with repatriation issues while employed at the Smithsonian Institution, quickly became a key advisor to the chief, and cultural resource issues became a prominent concern of the Duggan administration. During her four-year tenure, Harlan took the lead in archaeological consultations for the tribe and coordinated tribal involvement in a number of archaeological projects. The Cultural Resources Division also led the tribal council to incorporate wording and content from the North Carolina burial statutes and NAGPRA into the tribe's code to govern tribal policy on the treatment of native graves and repatriation issues.

One signal success of the Eastern Band's Cultural Resources Division was negotiation of a cooperative research agreement with Warren Wilson College concerning its archaeological field school at a late prehistoric village site on college property. The tribe officially sanctions the field school, and tribal members regularly participate in the fieldwork. The agreement also led to repatriation of human remains excavated at the site by the University of North Carolina. Warren Wilson College sponsored the tribe's interring of eighty-six sets of human remains in their original grave locations on college property.

In 1996, the Duggan administration led the tribe in the purchase of the old village site of Kituhwa, the great Mother Town of the Cherokee people. Acquisition of the 309-acre tract appealed to heritage-conscious Cherokees and practitioners of traditional religion, who view Kituhwa as the key shrine of Cherokee identity. The purchase, however, was driven by development-minded business people, who viewed the tract as prime riverfront real estate ideal for a tribal golf resort. As part of the planning process for development (or preservation), the tribe commissioned our group to conduct an archaeological inventory of the Kituhwa property. The core of the project area, a sixty-five-acre mound and village site, was already listed on the National Register of Historic Places, although tribal officials sought more precise definitions of site boundaries, content, and integrity, with a particular interest in identification or prediction of potential grave or cemetery locations. During the summer and fall of 1997, an archaeological team including Eastern Band members documented eleven archaeological sites at Kituhwa; these sites represent one of the largest and densest archaeological complexes in western North Carolina.

Eastern Band members frequently visited the crew in the field to check on our progress and findings. These visits apparently assuaged some initial suspicions, although they seem to have fueled others. We were repeatedly admonished by tribal preservationists to "do a good job" and "show what this place is," while development-oriented individuals appeared concerned about the extent of our findings. When I gave an interim report on the progress of the survey to the tribal council, I met a very different reception from my initial foray into council chambers seven years earlier. Although we served the Eastern Band under contract, we were introduced as the "tribe's archaeologists." Council members were cordial, even deferential, in soliciting comments and opinions about the site. When council members inquired about the potential presence of unmarked human graves on the property, our most conservative estimates had a sobering effect on the assembly. At the end of the session, the council thanked us for our efforts on the tribe's behalf.

Most of the tribe takes great pride in repossession of Kituhwa after 175 years; this pride is partially founded on the record of the tribe's history and prehistory contained in the site. The tribe's purchase of the Kituhwa tract reflects the economic empowerment of the Eastern Band with the influx of gaming revenues; it may also reflect cultural empowerment and a growing sense of optimism in the preservation and reclamation of tribal identity. In a 1997 rededication ceremony at the Kituhwa mound, speeches were couched in terms of "getting back what we had lost" and "becoming a whole people again." Visitors from Oklahoma related traditions that the Cherokees would regain Kituhwa in both real and metaphorical senses, but cautioned that if the tribe lost the site again, they would cease to exist as the Ani-Kituhwagi, the people of Kituhwa.

Commission of the archaeological inventory of the Kituhwa property signaled the tribe's assumption of responsibility for, and exertion of control over, archaeological resources linked to tribal heritage. For the tribe, these issues of responsibility and control are closely linked to tribal sovereignty and are exemplified by the recent development of an Eastern Band Tribal Historic Preservation Program, which supplants the jurisdiction of the North Carolina State Historic Preservation Officer on tribal lands. This program was instituted through the efforts of James Bird, a trained anthropologist and Eastern Band member; Bird's initiative sprang from conversations with Lynn Harland and is closely linked with Chief Duggan's institution of the tribal Cultural Resources Division. The current administration, headed by Chief Leon Jones, recognized the advantages of the proposed program and in July 1999 entered into an agreement with the National Park Service to create the Eastern Band of Cherokee Indians Tribal Historic Preservation Office. Bird, the current tribal historic preservation officer (THPO), oversees an ever-increasing number of consultations for the tribe; with the institution of new regulations in May 1999, federal and state agencies solicit comments from the tribe for actions in an area encompassing eight states. The THPO also manages archaeological resources on tribal lands and exercises oversight over all tribal undertakings.

The tribe's new stewardship of its heritage resources has faced an early test with the Kituhwa tract. The Eastern Band's Tribal Planning Office has entertained various land-use plans at Kituhwa, and in February 2000 hosted public meetings to elicit tribal members' feedback on options that ranged from preservation of the property in its current state to development of a golf resort or NASCAR racetrack. Public response weighed heavily in favor of preservation for religious reasons or from concern for the archaeological resources, although visions of commercial development at Kituhwa survived, and many tribal members believe the golf-course project to be a fait accompli.

In early April 2000, the site itself weighed in on the discussion. A tribal member who was preparing a garden plot at Kituhwa discovered human bones on a groundhog's spoil pile. The discovery, which graphically demonstrated the presence of graves at the site, was immediately reported in the tribal newspaper. Tribal officials determined that restoration of the remains to their original location was the appropriate remedy, and the THPO contacted our archaeological group to locate and expose the grave pit disturbed by the groundhog's burrow. We arrived at the site to find the groundhog hole cordoned off like a crime scene; a gallery of witnesses stood ready to monitor our work. Some of these witnesses were traditionalists determined that we should limit our excavations to the designated task; they also sought to shield us and others from any ritually damaging mistakes. Other witnesses were pro-development officials who suspected that the timely discovery of the remains might reflect a scheme to influence the Kituhwa discussion. Visiting officials voiced suspicions that the bones had been planted, and queried us as to whether the remains were human; if so, were they Indian, and did they represent tribal ancestors? Our mission thus shifted from a simple grave restoration to a politicized investigation of context and association for the disturbed remains. By the end of the day, we conclusively demonstrated that the groundhog burrow had passed through a grave pit associated with a fourteenth- or fifteenth-century Pisgah-phase midden. On the following day, traditionalists reinterred the remains as an act of ritual reclamation; a single elected tribal official attended.

Tribal members concerned with the preservation of Kituhwa hailed the exposure of human remains by natural forces as a divine message. Visitors who gathered around our excavation joked that the groundhog, Ogana, was the real tribal archaeologist, a *pro bono* digger immune from political influences. T-shirts proclaiming Ogana's role at Kituhwa appeared on Qualla Boundary within weeks of the reburial.

Most tribal members no longer perceive archaeology as inherently evil (or good, for that matter) but rather as a tool or methodology that can be used for or against tribal interests. During the public meetings on the future of Kituhwa, archaeologists were called upon by tribal members on both sides of the issue to report on the extent and importance of archaeological remains on the tract and to render opinions about the feasibility and advisability of development. When the groundhog's excavations at Kituhwa sparked further controversy, archaeologists were called in as arbiters expert in context and interpretation. Such solicitation of archaeologists' opinions by tribal members suggests major changes in perceptions of archaeology and its practitioners over the past ten years. Changes in tribal perceptions of archaeology have been largely event- and personality-driven. The return of college-educated tribal members to the reservation has created a proactive constituency for preservation and native-rights issues, and the election of a progressive, reform-oriented administration gave these elements a platform for expression. Through the agency of such individuals, the tribe has increasingly asserted proprietary interests in cultural heritage resource issues.

As archaeologists are recast as advocates for the preservation of cultural resources, their interests are increasingly convergent with those of the native community. In the course of numerous projects and consultations, archaeologists and Eastern Band members have come to recognize and appreciate the compelling interest and proprietary feelings of tribal members for the archaeological record of their own past. In turn, tribal members have come to recognize the validity of archaeological inquiry as a means to access components of their history that might be undocumented or unremembered. Eastern Band members who were once hostile to or dismissive of archaeology can now be heard to say, "We need our own tribal archaeologist," a Cherokee who can use the tools of Western disciplines to serve native interests.

Considerations of Context, Time, and Discourse in Identity Politics for Indians of the Carolinas

Patricia Barker Lerch

The comparative approach of anthropology is based on questions about how, why, and when individuals and groups have self-consciously formed, asserted, and adjusted their identities in response to context, place, and time. Self-consciousness develops in particular historical contexts of structured relations between groups and in contexts defined by certain political and cultural discourses (Skinner, Pach, and Holland 1989). For most of their history, American Indians in the Southeast have experienced tremendous pressures to assimilate, exerted by powerful defining ideologies that literally denied their existence. Nevertheless, many American Indians have struggled to preserve a sense of themselves as Indians. This struggle has involved individual actions and reactions, some passive and others aggressive. In the past, active resistance to those defining ideologies sometimes resulted in the powerful accommodating the views of the less powerful. For example, Blu's *The Lumbee Problem* (1980) chronicles one case in which people resisted the imposition of categories defined and held by those in power. The struggles and counterideologies offered by supposedly powerless peoples have effected a change in anthropology. In the past thirty years, some parts of the discipline have come under the influence of feminism, the Foucauldian understandings of the social construction of self, and the ethnohistorians' willingness to give serious attention to the narratives of American Indians (Fogelson 1974; Kan 1991; Skinner, Pach, and Holland 1989).

For anthropologists, the question now is how American Indians shape their identity and define themselves in relation to others. What role do others play in the game of identity politics? Anthropologists themselves have played an important role, especially in the last hundred years of Indian ethnology and history in the Southeast, because they are perceived as the experts. This paper, focusing on the events in the North Carolina Waccamaw Siouan Indian community in 1949 and 1950, addresses what anthropologists knew and how they worked with what natives knew half a century ago.

A LOST PEOPLE

On Monday, February 6, 1950, the Hon. Norris Poulsen of California, a member of the House Subcommittee on Indian Affairs, introduced a bill that would in effect recognize a "lost tribe of Indians in North Carolina." Poulsen had earlier described himself to John H. Provinse of the Bureau of Indian Affairs as having a vital concern with the rights of American Indians. A fellow Californian, James Evan Alexander, convinced Poulsen to sponsor the bill. Alexander first encountered the Waccamaw while visiting his wife's family; his first thought was simply to write a story or article about the troubled existence of the group, but he soon made friends with the people and became an active advocate for their cause. In 1983 I interviewed an elderly Waccamaw man, who recalled how Alexander helped the tribe by taking their cause to Washington. Alexander apparently believed that the Waccamaw descended from a mysterious lost tribe, long concealed in the swamps surrounding their homes. His passion for the tribe and his romantic convictions about their origins made an impression on those he met in Washington, where he gained a reputation for sincerity and honesty. Oliver LaFarge of the Association on American Indian Affairs praised the good fortune of the Waccamaw in finding such a strong friend, an assessment with which the Waccamaw leader Rev. R. T. Freeman clearly agreed.

Freeman is remembered as a "born leader," and stories about his involvement in community affairs make it clear that he had influence with powerful whites, which calls into question the "lost tribe" image. According to one story, Rev. Freeman was a close friend of North Carolina Governor Kerr Scott, whom he met through the latter's brother, a "bee man" who lived in the town of Bolton and for whom the young R. T. Freeman worked. Freeman apparently kept Gov. Scott apprised of

Waccamaw community interests. Eventually, he was officially appointed to designate who was and was not a member of the Waccamaw community. Interviews I conducted in 1990 confirmed that Freeman collected documentation in the form of birth certificates and affidavits certifying Indian heritage. State law in effect since 1921 sanctioned the practice of appointing screening committees that were responsible for certifying "Indianness" for the purpose of education in Indian schools located in Robeson County (Blu 1980:81).

Gov. Scott clearly recognized Rev. Freeman as Indian and made him the local judge of who else deserved that appellation. With this responsibility, however, came heartaches and headaches. One close associate of Freeman told me in 1990 that he "had the worse time of it, because he would have to tell some 'no,' [some] that was awful good friends, I mean you know it caused a lot of heartaches, you know, when you had a person that worked for you for twenty-five years and always got on good but was mixed blooded for some reason, then he had to [say] 'no, you're not [an Indian].'" When Alexander offered his help, Freeman therefore felt quite comfortable using an outsider to promote the goals of the community.

Freeman was widely recognized as the leader of the Indians living in the vicinity of Bolton, North Carolina. Letters in the Waccamaw Siouan Tribal Archives (WSTA) show that in 1943, Butler Prescott, Chief United States Probation Officer in the Eastern District of North Carolina, was assigned to conduct the pre-sentence investigation of several young Indian men charged with failing to report for military duty at the draft board in Whiteville. Prescott wrote to Freeman, informing him that his investigation led him to conclude that the young men were in fact Indians, and that efforts to designate them as Negroes and induct them into the military as such was the result of the prejudices of local white people. Freeman thanked Prescott for offering this testimony about the Indian identity of the young men and invited him down to go deer hunting. Freeman was thus clearly in touch with political leaders in the state capital, where the discourse on Indians favored granting authority to known Indians to act as gatekeepers of tribal identity. The key image was racial separation rather than that of a "lost tribe." An elderly man told me in 1983, "We was always conscious that we were Indian and . . . as a child coming up . . . I didn't think nothing of race being discriminated on from the whites and all, nothing like that. Because I was an

Indian, I was outstanding, and my folks were." Freeman may, however, have found the "lost tribe" image useful as he sought help from outsiders in furthering the Indians' cause.

In the fall of 1949, Alexander wrote to Julius C. Krug, Secretary of the Interior, asking that someone from the Indian office see a delegation from the Waccamaw. In a letter preserved in the Bureau of Indian Affairs (BIA) archives, Alexander explained that "the South's malicious practice of race discrimination recognizes only two sides to the color line. These Indians, though not wishing to be classed as white, refuse to accept classification as colored. This refusal to accept a destiny imposed on them by the white man has caused them to be the victim of many abuses." At their subsequent meeting with John H. Provinse, Assistant Commissioner in the Indian Office, the Waccamaw learned that the BIA'S programs were reserved for federally recognized Indian tribes. Provinse advised the delegation to seek help from North Carolina congressmen (Carlyle, Hoey, and Graham) who could draft legislation giving the BIA authority to aid them.

CATAWBA INFLUENCES

Alexander acted quickly following this visit to Washington, but he seemed discouraged. In a letter to a friend (Robert Ward of Rock Hill, South Carolina) that is preserved in the WSTA, he wrote: "The case of the Waccamaw Indians has been presented to the Office of Indian Affairs and they have been assured of as much assistance as the Bureau can offer them. . . . The amount of aid that [the Waccamaw] can be given without Congressional action appears to be quite limited." Alexander was seeking Ward's advice because the latter had been executive secretary for Senator J. P. Richards of South Carolina when the Catawba were seeking federal recognition. In fact, Ward's research on the Catawba had resulted in a brief historical publication (Brown 1966:17), and Alexander hoped to learn from the Catawba experience in gaining recognition. He asked Ward to send him a copy of the Catawba bill, constitution, and by-laws, which he would use to help the Waccamaw organize their case and make an effective presentation to the North Carolina legislators.

Neither the Catawba nor the Waccamaw ever had a treaty with the federal government, which meant that they were dependent on their respective state governments for assistance with education, health care, and economic development. The Catawba did, however, have a state reservation that provided them with some protection and recognition as Indians. South Carolina also provided the Catawba with some monetary benefits, although over the years the Catawba land base declined and their resources dwindled to almost nothing. Some found work off the reservation between 1900 and 1930, but the Catawba and their supporters still found it necessary to seek more assistance from the state and federal governments (Hudson 1970:81–86). In 1936 Richards got both levels of government to agree to offer support for agricultural assistance, industrial advancement, and social welfare (Brown 1966:354–55). In 1943 still more assistance was forthcoming when a "Memorandum of Understanding" was signed by the Catawba, the state of South Carolina, and the Office of Indian Affairs (Brown 1966:355–57; Hudson 1970:87–88). This memorandum provided for purchase of additional tax-exempt reservation lands that, along with the "old reservation" lands, were to be turned over to the Office of Indian Affairs to be held in trust. Furthermore, South Carolina promised that the Catawba would be made full citizens and would be allowed to attend public elementary and secondary schools as well as institutions of higher learning (which were reserved for whites at that time). Nevertheless, federally sponsored development initiatives, such as producing arts and crafts for sale, met with only limited success. Reviewing this era among the Catawba, Hudson (1970:89–93) concluded that the Catawba had gone so far toward assimilation that returning to a government-imposed agricultural communal lifestyle was very stressful. The fact was that intermarriage with whites opened the doors to white schools for some lighter-skinned Catawba. The "wardship" status won in 1943 created resentment in the white population because Indians had both privileges reserved for whites and a special tax-exempt status reserved for Indians. Tension resulted as the Catawba got caught between two opposing views, one of which held that independence, self-sufficiency, and acceptance meant intermarriage with whites and work in off-reservation industries—an accommodation that nonetheless exposed the people to discrimination and race prejudice. The other view defined Indians as people who depended primarily on communal agriculture on tax-exempt reservation land. Extra cash was earned by reproducing traditional arts and crafts for a non-Indian market. This had been a popular federal policy throughout the 1930s. A similar framework for definitions of "real Indian" history and social life also defined the context of the proposed Waccamaw Bill of 1950.

Ward advised Alexander and Freeman to contact the anthropologist

Frank G. Speck at the University of Pennsylvania, who could provide
information about the tribal origins of the Indians. Speck's research
among the Catawba since 1921 and his writings (Speck 1935, 1939) on
the Siouan tribes of the Southeast made him an authority on this region.
As he was preparing his manuscript on Waccamaw origins for the Indian
Office in Washington, Alexander corresponded with Speck, telling him
about the Waccamaw and asking his advice. Letters in the BIA archives
indicate that Alexander expressed his appreciation to Speck, whose
encouragement boosted Waccamaw morale. In a letter found in the
WSTA, Alexander told Ward that Speck's research established that the
group in North Carolina was "without a doubt" descended from the
Waccamaw, members of the Siouan nation, and closely related to the
Catawba. Alexander affirmed that the older members of the group
claimed to be part of the Siouan nation. In fact, in the 1930s some Indians from Robeson County had formed the Siouan Lodge of the National
Council of American Indians, Inc., hoping thereby to gain federal recognition as "Siouan Indians of Robeson County" under the Indian Reorganization Act of 1934; this action was widely known in Waccamaw
country (Blu 1980:82). Being known as Siouan Indians was therefore
not a new idea to the Waccamaw in 1949. The memories of older members of the group, who had clearly asserted their Siouan affiliation,
seemed to coalesce with the anthropological opinion about their likely
origins. In the fight for recognition, anthropological opinion became
very important, as it seemed to give scholarly sanction to the people's
oral history.

ASSOCIATION ON AMERICAN INDIAN AFFAIRS

The anthropologists and lawyers at the Association on American Indian
Affairs (AAIA) offered to help the Waccamaw cause. In December 1949
Alexander Lesser, AAIA's executive director, delivered a report on the
Waccamaw to his executive committee, which favored helping the Waccamaw as a way of furthering the mission of the AAIA. The Waccamaw
were described in the executive committee minutes as a "forgotten
group of Siouan linguistic affiliation" who were seeking recognition and
rights as American Indians, and the precedent of the Catawba was cited.
The executive committee passed a resolution that "the Association spon-

sor and/or support legislation to give Waccamaw Indians recognition as an Indian tribe and such rights as they be entitled to as a tribe, providing that proposed legislation meets the approval of the Waccamaw people." Lesser wrote to the Waccamaw via Alexander informing them of this action, and Felix S. Cohen, an attorney affiliated with the AAIA, discussed the wording of the bill with Alexander. The latter told Lesser that he was very appreciative of having "so fine and able a man" representing the Waccamaw interests.

Waccamaw leaders were seeking some type of wardship status, recognition as Indians, and protection from the federal government. The land under consideration (amounting to approximately 2,000 acres) included parcels ranging in size from 3 to 350 acres. Eighty percent of this land was described as swampy and unsuitable for cultivation. In a letter to Cohen that is preserved in the AAIA archives, Alexander described the land:

All of the good land adjacent to their present home has been taken by the whites, leaving them a few scattered islands in the swamps on which they reside. Not to be misled by the word island, it should be stated that these are merely patches of land rising only a foot or two above the water level of the adjoining swamp. During floods and heavy rains these so-called islands are inundated, thus destroying the season's crops. These floods are the rule rather than the exception inasmuch as the annual rainfall in this vicinity exceeds forty inches.

As noted above, the wording of the Waccamaw Bill had to meet the approval of the people, and so a petition, signed by 157 adult members of the community (described as representing "the entire adult population"), along with a resolution certified by the chief, R. T. Freeman, requested the legislation and was mailed to Lesser. Although there is no hint of dissent within the community in this communication, there had been a considerable amount of discussion.

Cohen had made two proposals to the Waccamaw, both of which would lead to congressional action giving federal recognition and some federal assistance. Alexander explained these proposals, the first of which suggested a bill for recognition of the Waccamaw as Indians and giving them the privilege of borrowing money from the U.S. government under the Indian Reorganization Act (IRA) of 1934. The IRA assisted tribes by helping them organize their governing bodies and write their own constitutions. It also granted them status as federally chartered corporations. As such, they were entitled to employ their own legal counsel and issue charters of incorporation for business purposes (Deloria and Lytle 1983:100). The result was a model of tribal government that followed the European legalistic form. In the Waccamaw case, accepting the model meant replacing an informal council of "men of age" who spoke for the major family groups with an elected tribal council, and changing the "chief spokesman" into a formal chief (Lerch 1992:59–60). The people rejected this proposal because they felt it would not accomplish anything but to "give their white county officials a nine-foot stick to beat them with," as Alexander wrote to Cohen in a letter preserved in the AAIA archives. Although both Cohen and Lesser favored this course of action, they acceded to the people's decision.

The second proposal, which the Waccamaw eventually adopted, outlined a procedure to place the Indian land in trust and to become wards of the federal government. Questions were raised about the transfer of land to federal trust status because their land holdings were small and the people worried about whether lands acquired in the future could also be put in trust. They also wondered whether putting their lands in trust under the federal government would indeed lead to the desired schools, medical attention, and other privileges accorded to federally recognized tribes. Alexander explained that federal protection would not necessarily create an ideal situation—certainly not in the short run—and there seemed to be growing concern about the meaning and consequences of accepting wardship status. An older man I interviewed in 1990 recalled this debate:

> At this time, we had our meeting at the church. There was some
> question about being wards of the government and being placed on a
> reservation. So we decided to let me go and look at this group in
> Rock Hill, South Carolina, that had just been made wards of the government. So we went and our finding was that the people looked like
> they had just quit working, sitting on the doorstep. So we didn't go
> for that and we came back and told [them] that that wouldn't work.

This 1949 visit was made to Samuel Taylor Blue, whom Speck called "the chief" of the Catawba because of his "unique personality and friendly cooperation with white friends and others seeking information" (Brown 1966:349). Speck had observed that Chief Blue maintained a traditional style of leadership and authority that surrounded him even when he was not the officially elected chief of the moment. Indeed, he served as elected chief for twenty years and as president of the Catawba for forty more. Even as a man in his seventies, he continued to lead his group. Blue's mother was a full-blooded Catawba and his father was white. He was Speck's key informant and invaluable to the research. According to Brown (1966:350),

> As chief of the tribe for many years he served the interests of his people by holding them together socially and politically to preserve their territorial and financial heritage from being dissolved. The climax of his administration came with the transfer of jurisdiction of the tribe from the state of South Carolina to the Office of Indian Affairs. . . . But Chief Blue's function as leader of the people . . . had been his lifelong endeavor to perpetuate the language and lore of the only tribally integrated group in the Southeast that spoke a language of the Siouan stock.

Blue understood his tribe's culture and traditions and he spoke the Catawba language. But to the Waccamaw visitors in 1949, it was his white appearance that was most impressive. My own informant remembers the visit:

> The first place we visited was Chief Blue's house. And [the federal government] built him a little, small wooden home. His son had on a new suit of clothes 'cause it was Christmas. He was carrying wood in . . . for a fire and it [was] right smelly with that new suit on. I said . . . to myself, how's these people think? Well, John D. Jacobs [one of the other Waccamaw visitors] he looked just like a white man, so [as a joke] we introduced him to Chief Blue as Chief Jacobs, 'cause both of them looked white. Actually by them being recognized and wards of the government, it showed us the picture. And we could see that regardless to what the government said we was in the white man's ways and it was time to accept the white man's ways. And that's what me and my family and most everybody else around have been going ahead and accept, being Indians, but working.

My informant's key issues were loss of independence and control over land and resources that had been earned through hard work over the years, and the idleness created by dependency on government handouts. This man was among the younger generation at the time. He recalled that when the idea of a reservation was proposed, "several men of my generation who had worked hard to get ahead . . . more so than many others who did nothing to help themselves, rejected the idea of pooling all of their resources so everyone owns everything in common." After visiting the Catawba of Rock Hill, these men were more against the idea than ever. They were, however, in the minority. He told me:

> When we had the meeting there was so many that was just thrilled to death because they wanted the reservation. But here's where I came in. I'd been out there stuffing from the time we got married. When we got married, we did not have any place to build a house. My folks didn't have nothing and her folks wouldn't give us nothing. And so there we was, kids without any land. We have worked hard, I loved sawmill work. But there was folks that had never done that in the community. They would take my land, take everybody's land and set it up as wards of the government. Each one of us would start with the same thing and I couldn't see that. From my personal feeling, not from my feeling whether I was an Indian or white, or what, I felt, what . . . am I doing? I am giving away all of this hard work—[that's what] I'm doing. And I had a cousin who had never in his life tried to do that and I used him in the talk that night. I said [my cousin] will have the same thing I got. He's got the clothes on his back and what he can steal. I got this land, this farm, new car, four or five trucks, thirty-two different people that works for us, and now I am going to come down and be a ward of the government and equal with him. I can't see that. And I got a few to seeing it my way.

Perhaps the language of the bill, which emphasized "voluntary conveyances" of land, reassured the people that they were not being forced to give up their land. Moreover, both Cohen and Lesser encouraged Alexander to try to persuade the Waccamaw that it was in their best interest to include the incorporation of the tribe under the provisions of the IRA. Indeed, the second section of the Waccamaw Bill did include this provision. Cohen pointed out that further aid might be forthcoming if the legislation were broadened to include the recognition provision.

Lesser noted in addition that the Waccamaw people were entitled to their rights under the IRA, and that it would be best if a single piece of legislation could accomplish this goal. Lesser feared that if the legislation were divided among several goals, it would never pass. In any case, the point was moot: the Waccamaw Bill was never enacted due to the opposition of the Office of Indian Affairs.

CONCLUSIONS

The "lost tribe" image obscured the active role of Waccamaw leaders, who shaped the course of their interactions with others based on their Indian identity. Within the state, politicians kept the "races" pure and separate by recognizing Indians like Freeman, who then passed judgment on those who qualified for special aid (e.g., Indian schools). Outside the state, politicians like Poulsen supported the Waccamaw Bill as a way to help Indians generally. Since they knew very little about North Carolina's definitions of racial groups, the "lost tribe" image stood as a logical explanation for why the Waccamaw were just then asking for federal aid as Indians. The AAIA anthropologists and Speck operated within the ethnology and history of the Southeast as it was understood in 1950. The Waccamaw were Siouan survivals, in their view, because they were isolated from the mainstream of assimilation. It apparently never occurred to them that Indian identity might also survive because Indians forged relationships within the political community. In this way, they actively resisted the defining ideologies of local politicians by balancing them against the ideologies of politicians in the state capital seeking to maintain the lines of racial purity that divided whites, Indians, and African Americans.

REFERENCES

Blu, Karen L. 1980. *The Lumbee Problem: The Making of an American Indian People*. Cambridge (U.K.): Cambridge University Press.

Brown, Douglas Summers. 1966. *The Catawba Indians: The Peoples of the River*. Columbia: University of South Carolina Press.

Deloria, Vine, Jr., and Clifford M. Lytle. 1983. *American Indians, American Justice*. Austin: University of Texas Press.

Fogelson, Raymond D. 1974. On the Varieties of Indian History: Sequoyah and Traveler Bird. *Ethnohistory* 2:1–18.

Hudson, Charles M. 1970. *The Catawba Nation.* Athens: University of Georgia Press.

Kan, Sergei. 1991. Shamanism and Christianity: Modern-Day Tlingit Elders Look at the Past. *Ethnohistory* 38:4–27.

Lerch, Patricia Barker. 1992. State-Recognized Indians of North Carolina, Including a History of the Waccamaw Sioux. In *Indians of the Southeastern United States in the Late Twentieth Century*, ed. J. Anthony Paredes. 50–72. Tuscaloosa: University of Alabama Press.

Skinner, Debra, Alfred Pach, and Dorothy Holland. 1989. Selves in Time and Place: An Introduction. In *Selves in Time and Place: Identities, Experience, and History in Nepal*, ed. Debra Skinner, Alfred Pach, and Dorothy Holland. 1–16. Lanham, Md.: Rowman and Littlefield.

Speck, Frank G. 1935. Siouan Tribes of the Carolinas, As Known from Catawba, Tutelo, and Documentary Sources. *American Anthropologist* 37: 201–25.

———. 1939. The Catawba Nation and Its Neighbors. *North Carolina Historical Review* 16:404–17.

Voices from the Periphery: Reconstructing and Interpreting Post-Removal Histories of the Duck Town Cherokees

Betty J. Duggan

REDISCOVERING AND INTERPRETING OBSCURED HISTORIES

Historical memory and sense of place and belonging are important aspects of local and regional identity for many people and communities in the southern Appalachian region. The proliferation of oral-history and public history projects and books by lay writers and academicians in the past several decades speaks to this interest. Such studies, however, do not always address methodological and theoretical questions. Whose history and which places, people, and events are remembered? What broader cultural and historical patterns and issues are embodied in historical documents and other forms of recording the past? How does one go about reconstructing histories of groups missing from or obscured in official historical records and received histories?

This paper summarizes highlights from the intersecting histories of Cherokees and non-Indians in the Ducktown Basin of southeastern Tennessee, as well as these Cherokees' relationships with other Eastern Cherokee enclaves between the 1840s and 1910s. It explores in particular my own search to recover and interpret supporting oral, written, and material documentation about this historic enclave which I call the "Duck Town Cherokees."[1] A much fuller treatment of this previously unstudied post-Removal Eastern Cherokee group is contained in my

Ph.D. dissertation (Duggan 1998a), which includes complete and extensive citations for various primary documents and oral-history accounts that cannot be included in this brief account. That study broke new ground in focusing on the Duck Town Cherokees at the analytical levels of community and family and as simultaneous participants in Indian and non-Indian societies and communities. The Duck Town Cherokee enclave is unique in another respect. It is the only post-Removal Eastern Cherokee group (and perhaps the only Indian group in the Southeast) whose members became laborers and participants in a local society created and driven by intense *in situ* industrialization prior to the Civil War.[2]

In approaching the reconstruction and interpretation of the history of the Duck Town Cherokees I was influenced by the theoretical approaches of three anthropologists noted for the study of the maintenance of indigenous and ethnic identities within plural societies. Wolf (1982) suggested that in order to rediscover institutionally muted or erased histories of indigenous peoples from the past five centuries of international market expansion one must look for local responses to processes of colonization and globalization. Wolf's sweeping study led me to think about the Duck Town Cherokees and their non-Indian neighbors and the economic and social arenas in which they both participated, and how these, in turn, were strongly affected by national and international interests and influences. Spicer's concept of persistent identity systems (1961, 1962) and Barth's distillation of ethnic identity as a unit of continuity in time (1969:11–12) convinced me of the powerful role that a sense of historic peoplehood and shared values can play in supporting a distinct group identity over time, despite dramatic changes in material and cultural circumstances.

The methodology of my dissertation research and of its final presentation was influenced by several traditional as well as experimental ethnographies, ethnohistories, anthrohistories, and folk and social histories (Blu 1980; Friedrich 1986; Hickerson 1970; Montell 1970; Price 1983, 1990; Spicer 1962; Wolf 1982). As the research progressed, I also found inspiration in the work of the pioneering French social historian Marc Bloch, who broke new ground with his methodological approach to the study of rural society. According to Bloch (1953:55–67), "It would be sheer fantasy to imagine that for each historical problem there is a unique type of document with a specific sort of use. On the contrary, the deeper the research, the more the light of the evidence must converge from sources of many different kinds." It therefore became necessary to adopt the standard historiograhic practice of subjecting each piece of evidence to both internal and external criticisms to test for authenticity, accuracy, and reliability (Gottschalk 1969; Kluckhohn 1945; Pitt 1992; Tonkin 1992; Vansina 1985). I ultimately utilized an array of primary and secondary sources and information-gathering techniques (e.g., oral-history interviews; ethnographic fieldwork; historic testimonies; local folklore; travelers' descriptions; earlier ethnographic, ethnohistoric, and historic publications; tribal, federal, state, and local records; photographs; and material culture) to locate and interpret evidence about the Duck Town Cherokees.

A final, critical factor in shaping my own approach was my previous and ongoing participation in several collaborative public humanities projects in southeastern Tennessee, and with Eastern Cherokees elsewhere (Duggan 1990, 1998b; Duggan and Riggs 1991). Some of my best leads and contacts cut across project boundaries and allowed me to gain access to previously untapped local resources. This work also made me aware that people who shared personal and family stories and local knowledge were really partners in my efforts as well as expectant audiences. In the end, it was the stories they entrusted to me that provided chapter frameworks and led to discussions of historical events and cultural issues.

PRE-REMOVAL CHEROKEE SETTLEMENT AND LIFEWAYS

The Ducktown Basin is a prominent, roughly fifty-square-mile geological feature that lies within the southeastern corner of Polk County, Tennessee, spilling over slightly into Cherokee County, North Carolina, and Fannin County, Georgia. This area is about eighty miles southwest of Cherokee, North Carolina, which is the tribal headquarters of the Eastern Band of Cherokee Indians; it is approximately fifty miles southwest of the smaller, culturally conservative Snowbird Cherokee community in Graham County, North Carolina. Because of difficult access and poor agricultural prospects, few non-Indian settlers initially bought the pennies-per-acre mountain lands opened up in and around the Ducktown Basin following the removal of the Cherokee in 1838. A decade later, when copper extraction became commercially viable, interest in the area increased quickly and dramatically (Barclay 1946; Duggan 1998a, 1998b; Ocoee District n.d.).

Eighteenth-century maps and settlement lists of the Cherokee country show no villages within a thirty-mile radius of the Ducktown Basin. In 1799 disbursement of treaty annuities to the village of "Duck Town" was mentioned in passing in a longer list of villages (Royce 1887), and during and after the American Revolution the floodplain and tributaries of the lower Ocoee River, some twenty miles west of the Ducktown Basin, became a refuge area for many displaced Overhill Cherokees (Lewis, Lewis, and Sullivan 1995).[3] My own preliminary genealogical and social network evidence raises the possibility that during the same period some Cherokee refugees from the war-ravaged Cherokee towns to the northeast and east may have retreated to the remote Ducktown Basin (Duggan 1998a).

An 1809 census of the Cherokees identified the village of "Wakoi Duck"[4] in this general locale; it had a population of 182 and had apparently seen some small influx of Euro-American trade goods, livestock, and agricultural and mechanical skills (Meigs 1810). My limited research into the pre-Removal Cherokee period of the Ducktown Basin's history turned up a published, early non-Indian oral-history account that linked a young Cherokee woman to a ceremonial event in the townhouse at Duck Town in the 1810s (Shamblin 1938). My investigations revealed that this woman, later known to local non-Indians as Granny Bird but whose Cherokee name was Cohena, played a central role in the regeneration of Cherokee society in the Ducktown Basin for more than four decades following the Trail of Tears (Duggan 1998a).

In 1835 the federal government conducted a comprehensive census and mapping expedition through the Cherokee Nation in anticipation of mandated emigration of the tribe to Indian Territory. Three principal settlements (Duck Town, Fighting Town, and Turtle Town) with a combined population of 312 were identified along tributary streams of the Ocoee in the Ducktown Basin locale, with smaller populations along several other nearby creeks. Preliminary perusal of spoliation claims later filed against the federal government by individual Cherokee residents of these (and other) communities for their losses suggests that between 1835 and 1838 the native population of the Ducktown Basin grew considerably as once again it became a haven for Cherokee refugees.

Social information about Removal-era residents and settlements revealed in an 1835 census roll that despite increasing acceptance or adaptation of aspects of western material culture and mechanical skills, Cherokees of the Ducktown Basin remained culturally conservative. Aside from the few ferry operators, no one there claimed familiarity with written or spoken English, although a good many could read the new Sequoyah syllabary. Several seemingly "nuclear" households, on closer inspection, actually included multiple adult farmers (male and female), indicating that traditional residence and land-tenure practices were still important. Regardless of personal circumstances or acculturation, all were forced from their homes by federal Removal troops in 1838, when they joined the infamous Trail of Tears to Indian Territory (Duggan 1998a).

FINDING AND DELINEATING THE DUCK TOWN CHEROKEES

While I was in consultation with a local museum prior to my Ph.D. studies, I heard about a Cherokee settlement in the Ducktown Basin ca. 1880. I found this account intriguing since the standard histories of the region and state suggested that Cherokee residence in Tennessee had ended with the Trail of Tears. Later, as I began my research, it became clear that primary information about the size, nature, and duration of this Duck Town Cherokee enclave was greatly obscured in or even missing from routinely consulted local, state, federal, and tribal documents. I was therefore surprised to find that oral-history recollections about specific, named members of the Duck Town Cherokee enclave had been passed down among several non-Indian families. These accounts provided me with important clues about individual Duck Town Cherokees and post-Removal settlement locations, as well as tantalizing glimpses of local interethnic relations spanning more than sixty years. Cherokee and non-Indian oral-history accounts balanced and complemented documentary evidence, yielding surprisingly rich detail about the Duck Town Cherokees and their everyday lives (Duggan 1998a).

My research ultimately identified three phases in the history of post-Removal Cherokee occupancy of the Ducktown Basin. The first phase, dating between the early 1840s and late 1860s, was characterized by settlement reestablishment, population expansion, and routine interethnic contact in several social and economic settings. It is ironic that despite this success, Duck Town Cherokees were absent from the 1840 and 1850 censuses, and were poorly represented in that of 1860. This period was followed by a phase lasting from the late 1860s to around 1885; it was characterized by shifting settlement location, population decline, more circumscribed interethnic relations, and increased involvement with another, previously unreported Cherokee enclave. The last phase, dating from the late 1880s to the 1910s, was a time of settlement retreat, social and geographical separation from local non-Indian communities, periodic settlement abandonment and reoccupation, escalating interethnic conflicts, and a final retreat to other Cherokee enclaves outside the area, including yet another previously unreported site (Duggan 1998a).

Tribal records, a petition generated from within the Duck Town enclave, and church minutes all document these trends. By far the richest ethnographic detail about community and family life of the Duck Town Cherokees, as well as about their economic and social relationships with local non-Indians and other Cherokees, was found through analysis of sworn pension testimonies from enclave members and non-Indian neighbors (Mullay 1848; Siler 1851).

First Phase

That the Cherokees were intent on returning to the Ducktown Basin was evident even on the Trail of Tears. A report filed by an army officer reported that at least twenty Cherokees from Fighting Town, under the leadership of a man named Chees qua (Bird), escaped from a Removal detachment, vowing to return to their homes.[5] I recorded one oral-history account and reviewed a deposition given by an Anglo-Cherokee who returned to western Polk County a decade after the Trail of Tears; both narratives suggest that a few Cherokees were never removed from Polk County at all. My research indicates that these people actually spent the immediate post-Removal years in neighboring Cherokee County. Comments in the first census of the Eastern Cherokee definitively place several families at "Duck Town" as early as 1844; they were under the leadership of John Chees qua (John Bird) by 1848 (Duggan 1998a; Hilderbrand 1908; Mullay 1848; Robinson 1838).

John Chees qua was recognized by other Cherokees as leader of the Duck Town Cherokees in the 1840s, and in subsequent decades at least two other Cherokee men were perceived by non-Indians as its leaders. A culturally more interesting and central figure emerges from interpretation of other records. It is a woman, the previously mentioned Cohena, or Granny Bird, who was probably a lifelong resident of the Ducktown Basin. She was John Chees qua's stepmother, and apparently his maternal aunt as well.[6] The widowed Cohena, her children, grandchildren, and their spouses formed the resilient core of the post-Removal Duck Town enclave throughout its duration (Duggan 1998a).

In 1851 a tribal enrollment named twenty Cherokees as residents of Fighting Town and Duck Town. By 1853 the local Cherokee population experienced dramatic growth and expansion of resettlement on the northern perimeter of the Ducktown Basin. That year at least seventy-nine Cherokees (eighteen families) were associated with the Duck Town and Turtle Town settlements, most with the latter. By 1860 all local Cherokee occupation shifted to Turtle Town, including most people who had first resettled at Fighting Town and Duck Town. Family relationships identified in tribal enrollments strongly suggest that traditional matrilineal kinship and matrilocal residence patterns were the organizing principles for all post-Removal settlements in the Ducktown Basin. Detailed information available about community life and personnel of the Turtle Town settlement demonstrates the culturally conservative nature of these communities with regard to language use, land tenure, labor groups, kinship obligations, and value choices (Duggan 1998a; Siler 1851).

Local non-Indians called the Turtle Town Cherokee settlement of this period "Bearmeat's Farm," after the Cherokee man who held legal title to a property of at least three hundred acres. Bearmeat (Yona chu whee yah) was the son-in-law and co-resident in a household that included the elderly Cohena, and he probably served as leader of the Turtle Town settlement during the 1850s and 1860s.[7] To its Cherokee residents, "Bearmeat's Farm" was communal land, occupied and farmed by four or five matrilineally related families, including at least three households with adult children of Cohena (Duggan 1998a; Siler 1851).

The practice of communal land tenure and agricultural work parties *(gadugi)* is historically well documented among the Cherokees (Fogelson and Kutsche 1961; Riggs and Duggan 1992). The so-called Bearmeat property actually had been purchased cooperatively ca. 1853, the money having been raised by pooling individual Siler roll disbursements, shares then being held by the families of contributors. In 1865 most or all of Bearmeat's Farm was sold to a non-Indian resident of Turtletown, and the money was distributed among the families. With the new owner's permission, the Cherokees continued to occupy and farm their old communal property as before until around the time of Bearmeat's death in 1869 (Duggan 1998a).

The Bearmeat's Farm Cherokee settlement, although traditional in organization and culturally conservative in lifeways, was physically and socially situated within the larger, dispersed non-Indian Turtletown community. From their cabins, the Cherokees could see non-Indian houses and farms less than a quarter of a mile away. On Sundays most attended the largely non-Indian Zion Hill Baptist Church, several non-Indian members of which had lived within or near the old Cherokee Nation. The church had sent a formal delegation all the way to Grassy Creek to witness to and bring the earlier Duck Town settlement members into their congregation. Some people from Bearmeat's Farm also hired out as day laborers for non-Indian neighbors and fellow church members. When one older Cherokee woman was abandoned by her husband, her Cherokee kin and local non-Indian women all tried to help by buying baskets and berries as she tried desperately to feed her family (Duggan 1998).

The determination exhibited by Duck Town Cherokees to recreate and sustain traditional community in their post-Removal locale was initially enhanced and then complicated and compromised by the discovery of world-class copper deposits in the Ducktown Basin in 1843 and then by the commercial development of those deposits after 1847. By the 1850s fourteen national or international mining companies were actively at work, and hundreds of laborers from the Appalachian region, other parts of the United States, and Cornwall in England were brought to the central Ducktown Basin. By 1860 as many as 1,000 people worked in the recovery, sorting, processing, and shipping aspects of the "Ducktown District" mining operations. Miners lived in rough camps or small settlements at or near each mine, and day laborers walked in from more distant farms and settlements (Barclay 1946; Duggan 1998b).

The sudden surge in the Ducktown Basin's Cherokee population between 1851 and 1853 was almost certainly due to the booming mining economy. It is still commonly known in the Turtletown vicinity that Cherokees in the mid-nineteenth century worked for a local timber man. On the other hand, the subsequent shift of Cherokee population to the Bearmeat's Farm settlement at Turtletown clearly reflects a desire on the part of enclave members to take up substantial communal agricultural lands and continue other aspects of traditional Cherokee life away from the bustling mining district. The visiting delegation from Zion Hill may have influenced their relocation as well (Duggan 1998a).

From the 1850s until possibly as late as 1878 when the mines closed for a dozen years, some local Cherokee men and boys, and other Cherokees who were said to have come down from North Carolina, worked alongside Appalachian counterparts as day laborers for local timber contractors who controlled the harvesting and processing of enormous quantities of timber into cordwood and charcoal to fuel ore roasting and smelting at the Ducktown mining operations. At least one entire Cherokee family—father, mother, and several children—supplemented their subsistence farming (the economic mainstay of Duck Town Cherokees, even those who also worked as hired laborers) as charcoal makers; the father and sons also worked as cordwood cutters. The family was headed by Chees qua neet (Jacob Bird), son of Cohena. They worked for food and clothing, not for wages, as did their non-Indian counterparts (Barclay 1946; Duggan 1998a, 1998b).

Although they worked and attended church together, and in most respects behaved as good neighbors, the Duck Town Cherokees and local non-Indians did not always enjoy easy relations during the first thirty years after Removal. There is some evidence to suggest ongoing underlying interethnic tensions. In the mid-1850s a petition signed by Polk County residents (few were from Turtletown) and a letter from a Turtletown man called for removal of all Cherokees from the county. There were repeated calls by some non-Indian congregants of Zion Hill for Cherokee members (all monolingual native speakers) to form their own church. One racially motivated crime did occur, but away from the area. The victims were the Mumblehead brothers, two young Cherokee Civil War soldiers from Bearmeat's Farm at Turtletown, killed in related, drunken attacks by non-Indian members of their own company. Although instigated by the company's notoriously vicious lieutenant, some of the soldiers were from the Ducktown Basin (and surrounding counties) and did return home after the war (Duggan 1998a).

Second Phase

The second phase (late 1860s to ca. 1885) in the history of the Duck Town Cherokee enclave is marked by population movement and decline, settlement dispersal and/or relocation, and increased involvement with a new Cherokee enclave in neighboring Cherokee County. Several families and individuals left the Ducktown Basin area temporarily or permanently, and only one Cherokee family continued to attend the Zion Hill church (and did so only sporadically) (Duggan 1998a).

After the Civil War, census records and sworn testimonies in pension records reveal that several individuals turned more steadily to work as agricultural day laborers in the employ of non-Indian farmers in the Turtletown District and for members of an Anglo-Cherokee extended family in a new Cherokee settlement called Long Ridge, about twelve miles to the northeast in Cherokee County, North Carolina. Around 1870 Walle yah Chees quah neet (Elizabeth or Betsy Bird)—mother, former charcoal maker, basket weaver and seller, abandoned wife, daughter-in-law of Cohena, and sister to James Cat—moved her family temporarily to western Polk County where a son worked as a laborer on a large farm owned by a non-Indian. Later in the decade they moved to Long Ridge, following her older children who were subsistence farmers there, and then back to Turtle Town to live beside her brother, James Cat (Duggan 1998; Hester 1884; Swetland 1868).

Sometime between 1870 and 1880 another daughter and son-in-law of Cohena, Sal ki nih (Sally Sr.) and James Cat (Tecosenaka) became the nucleus of a new Cherokee settlement in the Turtletown District, situated at the head of a remote cove at the base of Ditney Mountain. It was known locally as the "Cat Settlement," and its population probably peaked in 1884 with about nine families (thirty people). Since the Cat Settlement was located near the old Bearmeat's Farm, in which the Cats had been shareholders, it is possible that not all of that communal property passed out of Indian control in the late 1860s. Local non-Indians, however, recognized it as a separate settlement. In 1880 Cohena and the families of the two young Civil War widows resided with or next to the family of her daughter, Sal ki nih. A short distance away was a second cluster of Cherokee families, the Goings, Browns, and Longs. Households in both clusters were surrounded by the property and homes of non-Indian subsistence farmers, whose livelihoods and material wealth differed little from the circumstances of the Cherokees of the Cat Settlement (Duggan 1998a; Hester 1884; Swetland 1869).

I found little information in written documents or oral accounts about interactions and relationships between the Duck Town Cherokees and their non-Indian neighbors during this period. Several non-Indians who knew a number of local Cherokees well during the 1850s and 1860s, and who still gave sworn testimonies for them through the 1880s, had little knowledge of their activities after 1870. Non-Indian families around the Ducktown Basin have preserved a few stories about anonymous Cherokee women who traded baskets for clothing and foodstuffs in the 1870s. A descendant of a non-Indian neighbor of the Cat Settlement related a story about a female ancestor who learned to weave Cherokee baskets from women in the Cat family. Another non-Indian family tells of a male ancestor who hunted routinely with James Cat and other men around this time (Duggan 1998a).

The paucity of information about the Duck Town Cherokee enclave from all sources for this phase (especially the 1870s) undoubtedly stems from the fact that many of its members were mobile during this time of postwar hardship, making a living wherever and however they could. Two other critical—and for the Duck Town Cherokees related—external developments, however, had great import for the enclave during this period: the coalescence of the previously unreported Long Ridge Cherokee community, and the organization of the first Eastern Cherokee tribal council after Removal (Duggan 1998a).

In the 1830s the term "Long Ridge" referred to the curving, mountainous landform that shielded the historic Valley Towns on three sides. After Removal, this feature split the lands of old Cherokee County (now Graham and Cherokee counties) north and south. During the 1870s and 1880s, however, Eastern Cherokees also used "Long Ridge" to mean a dispersed Cherokee community on the larger landform in western Cherokee County; the members of that community were subsumed within several non-Indian communities, mostly in the Beaverdam District.

The Long Ridge settlement coalesced around the Anglo-Cherokee Smith family, prosperous farmers who had long lived in the area in the old Peachtree Cherokee community. Beginning around 1860 Henry Smith Sr. bought farms for his several children in the Beaverdam District. After the Civil War other Anglo-Cherokee families, their white relations, a few African-Cherokees, and a number of fullblood Cherokee families settled near the new Smith properties. Several families from the Bearmeat's Farm settlement at Turtletown moved there between the late 1860s and 1880s, including Bearmeat's widow, daughter of Cohena, who followed her own daughter (who had married a Smith son). Kinship ties (especially matrilineal ones), ability to speak the Cherokee language (at least minimally), and participation in Cherokee community life appear to have been important for this Indian settlement. Blood degree seems to

have mattered little, and even several non-Indian spouses spoke Cherokee. By 1880 only four fullblood Cherokee families in Cherokee county
lived away from Long Ridge (all at Tomotla). In 1884 Long Ridge had
twenty-one Cherokee households, six of them with ties to the Duck Town
Cherokee enclave (Duggan 1998a; Hester 1884).

During the 1870s and 1880s the non-Indian population of the Turtletown District had increased substantially and diversified as more farmers and professional and business people settled in what was still a
largely rural area. In this climate of social change and postwar economic
hardship, the safety of numbers, potential for marriage partners, and
presence of a Cherokee school in Long Ridge surely appealed to the
Duck Town Cherokee enclave. Even those who stayed in the Turtle
Town settlements maintained strong ties to Long Ridge and its residents,
especially the Smiths, several of whom served as interpreters and intermediaries for them with non-Indian officials between the 1860s and
1880s (Carrington 1892; Donaldson 1892; Duggan 1998a).

The Smith family was politically prominent during the formative
years of the Eastern Band of Cherokee Indians. Henry Sr. was described
by contemporaries as a "half breed" who had married a mixedblood,
Cherokee-speaking "Indian" woman. He had been an interpreter for the
pre-Removal Valley Town mission at Peachtree. At the first General
Council of the Eastern Cherokees, held at Cheoah on December 8, 1868,
one of Henry's sons, N.J. (Jarrett, or Tsa lahidi), served as the first clerk.
Another son, R.B. (Ross), was elected as one of Long Ridge's three
council representatives in 1870 (along with a Cat Settlement resident),
and Henry Sr. served for the Notla settlement. From 1880 to 1890 N.J.
was third principal chief of the Eastern Band and became a leading
informant on Cherokee history, folktales, and mythology for James
Mooney, the Smithsonian ethnologist. After N.J. and his family moved
to Cherokee, most Cherokees at Long Ridge began to leave. Resettled
Duck Town Cherokees returned to the Cat Settlement or moved to the
Nantahala River settlement that will be discussed below (Carrington
1892; Donaldson 1892; Duggan 1998a; Finger 1984; Hester 1884).

The Final Phase

The final phase in the history of the Duck Town Cherokee enclave (ca.
1885 through the 1910s) coincided with the turn of the century. This
period is characterized by settlement retreat, social and geographical

isolation, settlement abandonments and periodic returns, and final leave-taking. I gathered oral-history accounts from both Cherokee descendants and non-Indian informants; these materials suggest that ten unnamed Indians reported as residents of Polk County, Tennessee, in 1890 were the last members of the Duck Town enclave. Federal censuses between 1900 and 1920 report no Indians resident in either Polk County or adjacent Fannin County, Georgia. Nevertheless, I gathered at least a half-dozen oral-history accounts in different sections of the Ducktown Basin, all of which indicate that members of the enclave still lived in a mountain settlement at Turtletown as late as 1905. Elderly non-Indian informants in the southern end of the Ducktown Basin told me that a man and two families identified locally as "Indians" lived in the area into the 1910s, although none had clear ties to the Duck Town enclave (Duggan 1998a).

Sometime around 1885 James and Sal ki nih Cat moved from the Cat Settlement to the highest reaches of Little Frog Mountain, which towers over the valley around Turtletown to the east, the more distant Ducktown Basin to the southeast, and the broad Hiwassee River valley to the west. This final Duck Town Cherokee settlement at Cold Springs, as the place came to be known, was initially occupied by the Cat, Mumblehead, Walkingstick, and Bird families, and possibly a few others; it was, incidentally, the local Cherokee settlement first brought to my attention at the outset of my research. In this settlement, Cohena—mother, grandmother, aunt, and in-law to the core families that constituted the Duck Town Cherokee enclave for more than a half-century—probably passed her final days. The nearby place on this mountain called Granny Bird Gap still echoes her importance to non-Indian and Cherokee local history (Duggan 1998a).

By combining information from tribal community censuses, oral-history accounts by both Cherokee descendants and non-Indian informants, and church records, I was able to confirm that between 1888 and 1894 the shrinking Duck Town Cherokee enclave broke apart. By the latter date, all of the Cherokee families on Little Frog Mountain had shifted their permanent residences to a larger Cherokee settlement about sixty miles away in North Carolina. Several independent oral-history accounts indicate that several of the resettled Cherokees returned to the Cold Springs settlement, at least periodically, until around 1905. By the late 1890s returning Cherokees shared the mountaintop with a newly-wed white couple, and several families of mixed (white and "mulatto") race were living at Cold Springs, some in abandoned Cherokee cabins. These latter families are now said to have been "melungeons," a term that in the southern Appalachians has covered a range of socially marginalized, historic groups of mixed racial heritage; the term is now more common than the roughly equivalent "mulatto" of an earlier era. It is possible, given one surname, that they were mixedblood Cherokees who formerly lived in neighboring Monroe County, Tennessee (Beale 1972; Duggan 1998a; Kimsey and Portier 1982; Price 1953).

The short tenure of Cherokee settlements around Turtletown between the 1870s and 1890s is startling. For the first time since returning after the Trail of Tears, the Duck Town Cherokees appear to have followed geographical and social isolation as a means of self-preservation, a pattern adopted much earlier by other remnant Indian peoples in the East. This strategy stands out when viewed collectively and in light of a theme of violence that runs through several oral-history fragments recounted by Cherokee descendants and more detailed ones told to me by a non-Indian informant, who as a small boy frequently stayed at the home of one of the Duck Town Cherokee families on Little Frog Mountain (ca. 1905) while his father hunted ginseng with men of the Cat family and unnamed others. This period appears to be a time of almost constant retreat for the Duck Town Cherokees, until there was literally no other place to go within the Ducktown Basin (Duggan 1998a).

This phase of the Duck Town Cherokee enclave's history occurred at a time when racially motivated segregation and violence were open and aggressive toward African Americans and other minorities in the South (and elsewhere in the United States, for that matter). Indians were left in an anomalous middle ground in a racially polarized, black-and-white South. Between 1888 and the early 1900s railroad construction through the Ducktown Basin was initiated, resulting in the establishment of a large camp of African American laborers in part of the valley near Turtletown; heightened racial tension was thus brought to the doorstep of the Duck Town Cherokee enclave. Much later, when the railroad crew needed to work in the mining district, they were literally run out of the region one night by marauders, and their camp was burned to the ground (Barclay 1973; Duggan 1998a; Williams 1979).

Oral-history accounts preserved by Cherokee descendants, confirmed by the eyewitness accounts of one of my informants, leave no doubt that violence was prevalent in this era. A Turtle Town Cherokee man who had taken up residence with a non-Indian woman was murdered in ambush on his own front porch. James Cat was fatally shot by a non-Indian neighbor who mistook him for a wild turkey. Another Cherokee man fled after a fistfight with a non-Indian. The disappearance of a Cherokee girl remained unexplained. Violence culminated in a night-time attack on the family of Johnson and Sallie Mumblehead Cat at the Cold Springs settlement on Little Frog Mountain in the early to mid-1890s. A gang of non-Indian hooligans so terrorized the family with shooting and threats that they fled that very night to a Cherokee enclave on the distant Nantahala River in North Carolina, although Johnson managed to shoot one of the marauders. It is unclear whether the destruction by fire of the same family's cabin during one of their periodic returns ca. 1905 was deliberate or accidental (Duggan 1998a).

In the 1890s remaining members of the Duck Town enclave, as well as several of its temporarily resettled families at Long Ridge, rejoined at that same settlement on the Nantahala River, near Almond, North Carolina, about sixty miles northeast of the Ducktown Basin. Between 1890 and 1910, tribal census takers referred to this cluster of about twenty families as the "Nantahala Indians," recognizing them as distinct from the larger Cheoah settlement near Robbinsville, a dozen or so miles away. Despite access to larger farms at the Nantahala settlement, some resettled Duck Town Cherokees returned to their old cabins at Cold Springs periodically, perhaps even seasonally, for another decade (Duggan 1998a; Hester 1884).

The Almond locale was old territory for some of the first intermarried males of the post-Removal Duck Town enclave. Their birth families had been driven off farms on the Nantahala River when the state of North Carolina sold the land under the Treaty of 1819. The later Nantahala Indians' farms were inundated when dams were built in the late 1910s. Among the people forced to vacate were several third-generation Duck Town Cherokees and their young families; these people relocated together yet again, this time to a new tract of tribal land on Shepherd's Creek, just outside the largest Eastern Cherokee enclave at Cherokee, North Carolina. A few other resettled Duck Town Cherokees at Nantahala married into the nearby Cheoah settlement (Duggan 1998; Riggs and Duggan 1992).

INSIGHTS FROM THE PERIPHERY

At the beginning of this article I presented several basic methodological questions with which I approached location, recovery, and interpretation of sources and information for my research project, an historic ethnography of a previously unreported post-Removal Cherokee enclave. Drawn broadly from literature on ethnographic, ethnohistoric, and historiographic methods, these questions addressed what gets recorded or remembered as history, by whom, how it is remembered, and social and cultural encoding within received versions. This approach to sources also reflected the theoretical insights I gleaned from Wolf (1982), who suggests that formerly muted or erased histories of indigenous peoples may be rediscovered through examination of local responses to the processes of colonization and globalization. I was also personally committed to an ideal of informant collaboration and therefore saw the collection of oral history and other personal accounts as opportunities to give voice to native or local perspectives.

Following these precepts, my research project developed ways of understanding how external forces affected organization, personnel, and maintenance of the Duck Town Cherokee enclave. I also explored how and why the enclave's members responded as they did to changing social circumstances, and investigated the significance of timing of particular responses by members of the group. I found that by looking within, beyond, between, and sometimes around standard sources and (usually separate) treatments of Cherokee and Appalachian history and culture, I could gain extended glimpses into the lives and lifeways of members of the post-Removal Duck Town Cherokee enclave. I also found that historic biases in the generation and/or preservation of written documents left one often with partial, sometimes contradictory evidence, and, occasionally, false information about this community. To remedy this deficiency, it was necessary to scrutinize and analyze a variety of oral, written, and material sources together with broad cultural and historical frameworks.

Some scholars continue to debate the appropriate uses of oral traditions in historical reconstructions and interpretations, but few dispute their usefulness as mirrors of the social values, structures, and ideologies of the particular societies that recount them. As Vansina (1965: 170–71) states, "Each type of society has in fact chosen to preserve the kind of historical traditions suited to its particular type of structure, and the historical information to be obtained by studying these traditions is restricted by the framework of reference constructed by the society in question." This reminder is especially important when dealing with historical and social intersections of multiple cultural groups enmeshed in situations of colonialism and/or globalization, as in the case of the Duck Town Cherokees. The oral accounts collected in the course of my research were, with the exception of the detailed eyewitness accounts of one informant, usually brief, fragmentary, and passed down through several generations. Nevertheless, they still served as indicators of the kinds of activities and relationships that existed between local Cherokees and non-Indians during various historical periods. I found that information preserved by descendants of each group was complementary rather than overlapping in nature, especially as it reflected historic power relationships and interethnic conflicts. With the exception of the work of Finger (1984, 1991), there had been little published prior to my research about whether and to what extent Eastern Cherokees faced discrimination, racism, or overt hostility from non-Indians between Removal and the early twentieth century.

The Eastern Cherokees were not the only native people of the Southeast to escape Indian Removal. Indeed, after the shock waves of Removal subsided, two types of Indian communities with undisputed aboriginal ties remained.[8] First, there were tribes nearly decimated during the colonial era (the Tunicas of Louisiana and the Catawbas of South Carolina), which federal, state, or local officials and non-Indians in general assumed would die out. Second, there were remnants of removed tribes (e.g., Eastern Cherokees, Mississippi Choctaws, Florida Seminoles) (Paredes 1992; Peterson 1971; Porter 1986; Williams 1979).

The typical adaptive strategy for these surviving peoples was to establish homes or communities on marginal lands—inaccessible hollows, isolated mountain valleys or coves, ridge tops, scrub forests, swamplands—such that they would offer little in the way of direct economic competition or perceived physical threat to local non-Indians. In an ironic turn of events, this geographic isolation protected and strengthened the continuation of distinctive native social and ethnic identities (Beale 1972; Porter 1986; Williams 1979). Such an outcome would not have surprised either Spicer (1961:799) or Barth (1969), who both point out that oppositional processes ("we/they" dichotomies) play an important role in the formation and maintenance of ethnic groups ("persistent peoples"), often leading to the intensification of a sense of collective identity and a high degree of internal solidarity.

My research focused on the Duck Town Cherokees as simultaneous participants in local Cherokee and non-Indian society at the level of community, family, and individuals. I believe that the internal community formation and functioning of the Duck Town enclave probably typifies strategies of other conservative, post-Removal Cherokee communities, at least early in that era (Finger 1984; Hewes 1978; Neely 1991; Riggs 1999). Their experiences as part of an *in situ* industrialized local Appalachian society and economy, however, stand in sharp contrast to published accounts of other Eastern Cherokees and other native people of the Southeast prior to the Civil War.

During the first three decades after the Trail of Tears, coexistence and cooperation were possible between local Cherokees and non-Indians in several social and economic arenas. Through time, however, increasing social and geographical isolation of local Cherokees occurred, especially between the 1880s and 1910s, when the reinvigorated local copper industry drew heavily on imported labor at a time when ethnic and racial tensions were heightened throughout the South. As these changes occurred, Duck Town Cherokees forged stronger ties with other Eastern Cherokees and, through intermediaries from these groups, with an emerging tribal polity, the Eastern Band of Cherokee Indians. Exploration of these inter-community relationships led to preliminary reporting on two other previously unstudied post-Removal Cherokee enclaves.

As an ethnic minority in an emergent industrialized, class-based society, the Duck Town Cherokees' options were limited if they wished to continue residing in their home area. Members of the enclave were almost exclusively full bloods (phenotypically, genetically, and socially), native language speakers, and culturally conservative; as such, it was neither possible nor desirable to disguise their origins in order to "pass" in non-Indian society. Duck Town Cherokees, in fact, actively emphasized their unique ethnic and social identities in both public and private. At the point when that option was no longer locally viable, they withdrew into larger Cherokee enclaves in North Carolina, sometimes by choice, sometimes under the threat of racist antagonism.

Like Spicer (1961, 1962), Fogelson (1998:40) has stressed the basic rootedness of American Indian ethnic identities in "blood and descent, relations to land, and sense of community." Blu (1996) compares Lumbee Indian and non-Indian communities in Robeson County, North Carolina, suggesting that we should look for localized and historical meanings of "community" and "place of belonging." In cases where there are complicated ethnoscapes, as with the Lumbee or the historic Duck Town Cherokees, community may be in evidence as socially distinctive but not necessarily geographically separate entities. This situation reminds us of Wolf's admonition to study the effects of colonialization and globalization on local groups. The determination of the Duck Town Cherokees to remain in the Ducktown Basin despite extensive social and environmental changes, physical containment of their settlements, and increasingly overt hostility demonstrates that strong, longstanding definitions of social community and locale were central to their sense of Cherokee identity. After all, the Duck Town Cherokees did not randomly disperse as families or individuals into other Cherokee enclaves when they left the Ducktown Basin locale; rather, they resettled together repeatedly. Such action strongly suggests that their primary sense of group identity was based on an ancient, localized social community (e.g., a dispersed village based on matriliny and matrilocality, and/or alliances between particular matrilineages or sets of villages) denoted and embodied at specific times and locations by the place/group names Duck Town, Fighting Town, Turtle Town, and Nantahala Indians. This ancient social "community" was remembered and rooted for more than a century in the geographic locale known to Cherokees as "Duck Town," carrying forward the name of the area's first recorded Cherokee village, whose antecedents probably go back to the pre-Revolutionary Cherokee Middle or Valley Town.

The Duck Town Cherokee enclave is thus an example of a persistent identity system (à la Spicer) or of a unit of continuity through time (à la Barth). This pattern of resilient localized identity fits with the findings of Gearing (1962) and Gilbert (1943), who pointed out that, under ordinary circumstances, early historic Cherokee life was about village loyalties and that villages were organized around kinship, often with one or more matrilineages predominating. Mooney (1900) and Schroedl (1986, 1989) noted the routine, periodic relocation of early historic Cherokee villages to fresh agricultural lands; they also point to the maintenance of distinct social and ethnic communities within several historic host Cherokee settlements or regions after wholesale displacements by war or other disasters.

My dissertation research intersected with the local histories of the larger Qualla (Cherokee, North Carolina) and Cheoah Cherokee post-Removal enclaves, demonstrating a similar pattern of localized identity that stood against the effects of the chaos and massive displacements of Removal. I therefore think that further historical studies of Eastern Cherokee communities will reveal that rather than passively accepting the guidance and mandates, or relying on the benevolence, of external forces and people, as some historical accounts have implied, most culturally conservative post-Removal Eastern Cherokees at the level of settlement and/or neighborhood actively and immediately set about to restore ordinary life through traditional ways of making and keeping community.

Among culturally conservative Cherokee groups, such as the post-Removal Duck Town enclave, these ancient senses of group activity carried forward, sometimes through repeated displacements in the nineteenth and twentieth centuries, and in later years coexisted with an evolving sense of Eastern Cherokee tribal identity. The rich, layered nature of Eastern Cherokee identity was brought home pointedly to me by one Duck Town Cherokee descendant, the late Paul Catt, who replied when I first asked him for the names of other descendants, "We're all from there." While long gone from a specific geographic locale, the Duck Town Cherokee enclave endures.

NOTES

I am grateful to Rubie Watson, Howells Director of the Peabody Museum of Archaeology and Ethnology of Harvard University and supervisor of my recent postdoctoral fellowship at that institution, for time to develop the conference paper and initial draft of this article. I owe a great debt to my Ph.D. dissertation chair at the University of Tennessee, Benita Howell, who introduced me to the classic literatures on ethnicity and ethnohistory, and to Faye Harrison, of the same institution, whose History in Anthropology course brought me to other relevant literatures and debates. Both greatly influenced the dissertation from which this article derives. Other scholars (especially Brett Riggs), institutions, family and friends, and friends from Ducktown Basin (especially the late George Mealer and Alga B Kimsey) and the Eastern Cherokees (especially the late Paul Catt and Doris and Marina Catt) are thanked by name in my dissertation. Miles Richardson and Bill and Sharon Davidson of Louisiana State University have most recently ensured that I have pleasant writing accommodations and resources. I thank Terry Faulkner for kindly and ably preparing the maps for my dissertation. Finally, I thank Lisa Lefler for encouraging my participation in this volume and for her patience with delays as I shuttled among several field locations.

1. I refer to Cherokees who resettled the Ducktown Basin after the Trail of Tears as the "Duck Town Cherokees" (or, alternately, Duck Town enclave) because the earliest tribal census (Thomas 1840) lists all Cherokees living there as living at "Duck Town," even though other sources (Siler 1851) indicate that they resided in two geographically distinct clusters by that date. Duck Town was also the name of the first recorded pre-Removal Cherokee settlement in this locale. I have retained the pre-Removal spellings of "Turtle Town" and "Fighting Town," as did some tribal documents. Throughout this article, I use the spellings "Ducktown," "Fightingtown," and "Turtletown" to mean the post-Removal communities or neighborhoods that were not controlled by Indians.

2. Dunaway (1996) discusses in detail Cherokee involvement in the early-eighteenth-century deerskin trade, presenting independent native hunters, skin preparers, and traders as peripheral workers in an international fur and hide industry. Other Cherokees were similarly engaged as workers in an early international ginseng trade. Duggan (1998b) follows up briefly on this topic with specific regard to Cherokees in southeastern Tennessee. Native participation in an *in situ* heavy industry prior to the Civil War has not been previously reported in the Southeast, although local legend has it that in the early nineteenth century Cherokees operated an iron furnace at Tellico Plains, Tennessee (then Great Tellico), about twenty miles north of Turtle Town (Duggan 1998b). Many Cherokee men and boys from the Qualla settlements at Cherokee and the Cheoah (Snowbird) settlement worked as loggers between the 1880s and 1930s, when the virgin and then the second-growth forests of this part of the southern Appalachians were first harvested commercially on a large scale (Duggan 1998b; Finger 1984, 1991; Neely 1991).

3. "Wakoi" is an early transliteration of a Cherokee word now rendered "Ocoee" in English. The pre-Removal village of Duck Town was situated near the Ocoee River on one or more small tributary streams (several of them southwest of the modern community of Ducktown). It may have been relocated at least once between 1799 and 1838.

4. In the eighteenth century Cherokee villages were clustered in four distinct locales referred to by the British as the Lower, Valley, Middle, and Overhill Towns, situated respectively on the headwaters of the Savannah, Hiwassee, Tuckasegee, and Little Tennessee rivers.

5. I am thankful to Brett Riggs for sharing this account found during his dissertation research in Removal-era primary documents, and for providing me with a typed transcript.

6. Sororal polygyny is not uncommon among matrilineal societies. It was noted occasionally among the historic Cherokees (Gilbert 1943; Mooney 1900) and, perhaps, in rare instances in modern times.

7. Bearmeat's wife Elizabeth (Leshe or Si sih) is incorrectly identified as

Cohena's granddaughter, rather than her daughter, in one tribal enrollment. She was a sister to Chees qua neet (Jacob Bird) and Sal ki nih (Sally Cat Sr.), who were identified as children of Cohena by members of the Duck Town enclave.

8. Examination of the topic of historic social groups in the Southeast that claimed or were ascribed some native ancestry is beyond the scope of this article. The reader is referred to Beale (1972), Blu (1980), Paredes (1992), Porter (1986), and Williams (1979) for an introduction to this literature.

REFERENCES

Works Cited

Barclay, R. E. 1946. *Ducktown Back in Raht's Time*. Chapel Hill: University of North Carolina Press.

———. 1973. *The Railroad Comes to Ducktown*. Knoxville, Tenn.: Cole Printing and Thesis Service.

Barth, Fredrik. 1969. *Ethnic Groups and Boundaries: The Social Organization of Culture Difference*. London: George Allen and Unwin.

Beale, Calvin L. 1972. An Overview of the Phenomenon of Mixed Racial Isolates in the United States. *American Anthropologist* 74(3):704–9.

Bloch, Marc. 1953. *The Historian's Craft*. New York: Knopf.

Blu, Karen. 1980. *The Lumbee Problem: The Making of an American Indian People*. Cambridge, U.K.: Cambridge University Press.

———. 1996. "Where Do You Stay At?" Home Place and Community among the Lumbee. In *Senses of Place*, ed. S. Feld and K. H. Basso. 197–227. Santa Fe, N.M.: School of American Research Press.

Carrington, Henry B. 1892. Eastern Band of Cherokees in North Carolina. In *The Extra Census Bulletin: Indian—Eastern Band of Cherokees of North Carolina*, ed. T. Donaldson. 11–21. Washington, D.C.: U.S. Census Printing Office.

Donaldson, Thomas. 1892. Statistics of Indians: Eastern Band of Cherokees of North Carolina and Eastern Cherokees. In *The Extra Census Bulletin: Indian—Eastern Band of Cherokees of North Carolina*, ed. T. Donaldson. 7–10. Washington, D.C.: U.S. Census Printing Office.

Duggan, Betty J. 1990. New Ways for Old: Assessing Contributions of the Tennessee Community Heritage Project. In *Cultural Heritage Conservation in the American South*, ed. B. Howell. 54–65. Athens: University of Georgia Press.

———. 1998a. *Being Cherokee in a White World: The Ethnic Persistence of a Post-Removal American Indian Enclave*. Ph.D. dissertation, University of Tennessee.

————. 1998b. *From Furs to Factories: Exploring Historic Industrialization in the Tennessee Overhill.* Etowah, Tenn.: Tennessee Overhill Heritage Association.

Duggan, Betty J., and Brett H. Riggs. 1991. Cherokee Basketry: An Evolving Tradition. In *Studies in Cherokee Basketry*, ed. B. Duggan and B. Riggs. 22–52. Knoxville: Frank H. McClung Museum, University of Tennessee.

Dunaway, Wilma A. 1996. *The First American Frontier: Transition to Capitalism in Southern Appalachia, 1700–1860.* Chapel Hill: University of North Carolina Press.

Finger, John R. 1984. *The Eastern Band of Cherokees 1819–1900.* Knoxville: University of Tennessee Press.

————. 1991. *Cherokee Americans: The Eastern Band of Cherokees in the Twentieth Century.* Lincoln: University of Nebraska Press.

Fogelson, Raymond D. 1998. Perspectives on Native American Identity. In *Studying Native America: Problems and Prospects*, ed. R. Thornton. 40–59. Madison: University of Wisconsin Press.

Fogelson, Raymond D., and Paul Kutsche. 1961. Cherokee Economic Cooperatives: The *Gadugi*. In *Symposium on Cherokee and Iroquois Culture*, ed. W. Fenton and J. Gulick. 83–123. Washington, D.C.: Smithsonian Institution, Bureau of American Ethnology.

Friedrich, Paul. 1986. *The Princes of Naranja: An Essay on Anthrohistorical Method.* Austin: University of Texas Press.

Gearing, Frederick O. 1962. *Priests and Warriors: Social Structures for Cherokee Politics in the Eighteenth Century.* Menasha, Wis.: American Anthropological Association.

Gilbert, William H. 1943. *The Eastern Cherokees.* Washington, D.C.: Smithsonian Institution, Bureau of American Ethnology.

Gottschalk, Louis R. 1969. *Understanding History: A Primer of Historical Method.* New York: Knopf.

Hester, Joseph G. 1884. *Census of the Eastern Cherokees.* Washington, D.C.: United States National Archives.

Hewes, Leslie. 1978. *Occupying the Cherokee Country of Oklahoma.* Lincoln: University of Nebraska Press.

Hickerson, Harold. 1970. *The Chippewas and Their Neighbors: A Study in Ethnohistory.* New York: Holt, Rinehart and Winston.

Hilderbrand, John W. 1908. *Some Recollections of Jack Hilderbrand as Dictated to Jack Williams, Esq., and M. O. Cate.* Nashville: Tennessee State Library and Archives.

Kimsey, Alga B, and Carolyn Portier. 1982. *The Kimsey Family: A Journey to Tennessee.* Lakemont, Ga.: Copple House Books.

Kluckhohn, Clyde. 1945. The Personal Document in Anthropological Science. In *The Use of Personal Documents in History, Anthropology, and Sociology,*

ed. L. Gottschalk, C. Kluckhohn, and R. Angell. 164–173. New York: Social
    Science Research Council.

Lewis, Thomas M. N., Madeline Kneberg Lewis, and Lynne P. Sullivan. 1995.
    The Prehistory of the Chickamauga Basin in Tennessee. Knoxville: Univer-
    sity of Tennessee Press.

Meigs, Return J. 1810. *A General Statistical Table of the Cherokee Natives*.
    Winston-Salem, N.C.: Moravian Archives.

Montell, William Lynwood. 1970. *The Saga of Coe Ridge: A Study in Oral His-
    tory*. Knoxville: University of Tennessee Press.

Mooney, James. 1900. *Myths of the Cherokee*. Washington, D.C.: Smithsonian
    Institution, Bureau of American Ethnology.

Mullay, John C. 1848. *Census of the Eastern Cherokees*. Washington, D.C.:
    United States National Archives.

Neely, Sharlotte. 1991. *Snowbird Cherokees: People of Persistence*. Athens:
    University of Georgia Press.

Ocoee District. n.d. *Ocoee District Land Records*. Nashville: Tennessee State
    Library.

Paredes, J. Anthony. 1992. *Indians of the Southeastern United States in the Late
    Twentieth Century*. Tuscaloosa: University of Alabama Press.

Peterson, John H. 1971. The Indians in the Old South. In *Red, White, and Black:
    Symposium on Indians in the Old South*, ed. C. Hudson. 116–33. Athens:
    University of Georgia Press.

Pitt, David C. 1992. *Using Historical Sources in Anthropology and Sociology*.
    New York: Holt, Rinehart and Winston.

Porter, Frank W. 1986. *Strategies for Survival: American Indians in the East-
    ern United States*. Westport, Conn.: Greenwood Press.

Price, Edward T. 1953. A Geographic Analysis of White-Indian-Negro Racial
    Mixtures in the Eastern United States. *Annals of the Association of Ameri-
    can Geographers* 43:138–55.

Price, Richard. 1983. *First-Time: The Historical Vision of an Afro-American
    People*. Baltimore: Johns Hopkins University Press.

———. 1990. *Alabi's World*. Baltimore: Johns Hopkins University Press.

Riggs, Brett H. 1999. *Removal Period Cherokee Households in Southwestern
    North Carolina: Material Perspectives on Ethnicity and Cultural Differenti-
    ation*. Ph.D. dissertation, University of Tennessee.

Riggs, Brett H., and Betty J. Duggan. 1992. *The Catt Family: A Case Study in East-
    ern Cherokee History*. Washington, D.C.: Smithsonian Institution, National
    Museum of American History, Department of Social and Cultural History.

Robinson, Joseph. 1838. *Correspondence of the Eastern Division Pertaining to
    Cherokee Removal*. Washington, D.C.: United States National Archives.

Schroedl, Gerald F. 1986. *Overhill Cherokee Archaeology at Chota-Tanasee*.

Knoxville: University of Tennessee, Department of Anthropology.

———. 1989. Overhill Cherokee Household and Village Patterns in the Eighteenth Century. In *Proceedings of the Twenty-first Annual Conference of the Archaeological Association of the University of Calgary*, ed. S. MacEachern, D. Archer, and R. Garvin. 350–60. Calgary: University of Calgary Archaeological Association.

Shamblin, John S. 1938. History and Legendary Story of the Frog Mountain. *Polk County News*, June 23: 3–4.

Siler, David W. 1851. *Census of the Eastern Cherokees*. Washington, D.C.: United States National Archives.

Spicer, Edward H. 1961. Types of Contact and Processes of Change. In *Perspectives in American Indian Culture Change*, ed. E. Spicer. 517–44. Chicago: University of Chicago Press.

———. 1962. *Cycles of Conquest: The Impact of Spain, Mexico, and the United States on the Indians of the Southwest, 1533–1960*. Tucson: University of Arizona Press.

Swetland, Silas H. 1869. *Census of the Eastern Cherokees*. Washington, D.C.: United States National Archives.

Thomas, William Holland. 1840. *Census of the North Carolina Cherokees*. Durham, N.C.: Duke University, Special Collections Library.

Tonkin, Elizabeth. 1992. *Narrating Our Pasts: The Social Construction of Oral History*. Cambridge, U.K.: Cambridge University Press.

Vansina, Jan. 1985. *Oral Tradition: A Study in Historical Methodology*. London: Routledge and Kegan Paul.

Williams, Walter L. 1979. *Southeastern Indians Since the Removal Era*. Athens: University of Georgia Press.

Wolf, Eric. 1982. *Europe and the People without History*. Berkeley: University of California Press.

Additional Archival Materials

Cherokee Indian Agency. 1894–1910. Censuses of Cherokee Communities. Administrative Records, Enumeration and Enrollment Records. Records of the Bureau of Indian Affairs. Record Group 75. Federal Records Center, East Point, Georgia.

Cherokee Indian Agency. 1898. Statistics of Birdtown and Nantahala Indians, June 1898. Administrative Records, Enumeration and Enrollment Records. Records of the Bureau of Indian Affairs. Record Group 75. Federal Records Center, East Point, Georgia.

Cherokee Indians of Polk County. 1853. Petition from the Cherokee Indians of Polk County, Tennessee, to the President of the United States. Letters

Received by the Office of Indian Affairs. Records of the Bureau of Indian Affairs. Record Group 75. Microcopy 234. United States National Archives, Washington, D.C.

Cherokee Property Valuations. 1836–1837. Valuations of Cherokee Property in North Carolina. Bureau of Indian Affairs. Record Group 75. United States National Archives, Washington, D.C.

Fourth Board of Cherokee Commissioners. 1846–1847. Records of the Fourth Board of Cherokee Commissioners. Claim Papers. Record Group 75. United States National Archives, Washington, D.C.

Henderson Enrollment. 1835. Census Roll of the Cherokee Nation. Records of the Bureau of Indian Affairs. Record Group 75. United States National Archives, Washington, D.C.

Miller, Guion. 1906–1910. Report of Enrollment, with exhibits (1909) and Supplemental Report (1910). Records of the Bureau of Indian Affairs. Microcopy m685. United States National Archives, Washington, D.C.

Mills, William. 1857. William Mills to U.S. Government, July 2, 1857. Records of the Bureau of Indian Affairs. Record Group 75. Microcopy 234. United States National Archives, Washington, D.C.

Penelope Allen Cherokee Collection. Microfilm Record 151. Tennessee State Library and Archives, Nashville.

Polk County Citizens. 1855. Petition to the State of Tennessee to Remove "The Cherokee Indians" of Polk County, Tennessee. Manuscript on file, Tennessee State Library and Archives, Nashville.

Thomas, William Holland. 1837–1842. Miscellaneous Day, Cash and Account Books. William Holland Thomas Papers, Special Collections Library, Duke University, Durham, N.C.

United States Bureau of the Census, Department of Commerce. 1910. *Indian Population in the United States and Alaska, 1910*. Washington, D.C.: U.S. Government Printing Office.

———. 1840–1920. Sixth to Fourteenth U.S. Censuses, Population, Agricultural, and Mortality Schedules: Cherokee County, North Carolina; Fannin County, Georgia; Graham County, North Carolina; Monroe County, Tennessee; Polk County, Tennessee. Microfilm.

United States Military Records, Civil War Pension Files. n.d. Miscellaneous Depositions, Pension Application Files. Military Records. United States National Archives, Washington, D.C.

Zion Hill Baptist Church. n.d. Minutes, Books A and B. Manuscripts on file, Zion Hill Baptist Church, Turtletown, Tennessee.

Curating Our Past:
Museum Direction Driven
by Tribal Perspectives

Russell G. Townsend

Throughout much of the nineteenth and twentieth centuries, museums of culture history have been organized and operated largely by western collectors and antiquarians and have been dominated by displays of material culture (Alexander 1993:86). Items from all over the world have been organized in some thematic way, often with identifying labels displaying names, regions, and dates. Many of these items, especially those representing prehistoric cultures, remained poorly understood, their possible functions often the object of wild speculation resulting in erroneous conclusions. Alexander documents the development of the culture-history approach in museum exhibition, but he fails to document the severe criticisms this approach has received from many anthropologists since the 1950s. Kuper (1988) offers a thorough examination of the shortcomings of the culture-history approach used by anthropologists during the nineteenth and early twentieth centuries, and which is still used in far too many museums even today. All of us have seen numerous museum exhibits with cases of curious objects labeled "lithic artifact, probable ceremonial function." Misrepresentations of many artifacts result from a Eurocentric bias, which invented and maintains concepts of "primitive society" in order to maintain the image of the dominance of European culture (Kuper 1988:8). It has been perhaps the height of our arrogance to gather Native American objects, display them to the world, and, with little regard for our ignorance, proclaim them to be "thus and so, used in this or that way."

A few attempts were made in the latter part of the nineteenth century to gather detailed ethnographic accounts that might provide analogous insight into these disparate material collections, an approach that continued through the twentieth century, meeting with varying degrees of success. On the whole, these attempts have been too few and too seldom fully applied. Museum curators often seem more interested in preservation techniques and collection enhancement than in applying anthropological accounts that would allow museum objects to tell a more complete cultural story. Some Native Americans, frustrated by the lack of depth in many exhibits, started to construct their own museums.

Ever since the 1920s, Native Americans have shown a real interest in developing museums of their own that display their cultures. A tribal museum is defined simply as "a museum owned and operated by a tribe" but that may also reflect the following criteria, which also apply:

> Included are museums/centers operated in urban sites by conglomerate groups of Native Peoples; museums/centers managed by American Indian tribal entities; museums operated by American Indian individuals; and, finally, museums financed by non-tribal monies but located within tribal communities and hiring or partnering with residents of the community or otherwise viewed as presently serving as a "tribal museum" (Center for Museum Studies 1998:6).

The museums discussed in this essay adhere to these criteria. The Bureau of Indian Affairs identifies more than 500 tribal entities in the United States; there are 154 recognized tribal museums or cultural centers in the United States and Canada, a figure that is expected to double in the near future and continue growing into the twenty-first century (Center for Museum Studies 1998:6).

Many of the early tribal museums were created with private funding: a number of individuals from various tribal entities would donate money to support the construction of a museum that reflected a tribal perspective. For example, a private museum was opened in 1948 by Mr. and Mrs. Samuel E. Beck. "Some fifty thousand artifacts" in their collection were purchased in 1952 by the Cherokee Historical Association (Finger 1993:138), which in 1977 turned over its administration to the re-named Museum of the Cherokee Indian to the tribal council of the Eastern Band (Finger 1993:154–5).

The Museum of the Cherokee Indian, located in Cherokee, North Carolina, on the Qualla Boundary, told the Cherokee story through text, graphics, and artifacts. The exhibit, however, still focused on the material culture, and largely relied on the expertise of white archaeologists. Moreover, the objects in the museum were collected and displayed with a European bias. As the museum cultivated more Cherokee benefactors, the Cherokee found that they had a larger voice in determining and designing exhibits, although the system still leaves many tribal members unsatisfied.

The American Indian revival movement of the 1960s and 1970s encouraged many groups to tell their own stories in their own voices. Popular films such as *Billy Jack* and *Little Big Man*, coupled with a greater awareness of environmental concerns, led the American public at large to idealize Native Americans as master environmentalists. Indians across North America continue to enjoy the benefits—and suffer some of the losses—occasioned by these exaggerated images. Some tribal entities took advantage of the new climate by developing museum concepts that would allow them to present an Indian perspective on their collections and at the same time bolster depressed economies in their regions (King 1988:11).

A group of full and mixedblood Oklahoma Cherokees in 1964 banded together to create the Cherokee Historical Society, an entity dedicated to the preservation and explanation of their culture. Using private donations and grant monies, they developed the Cherokee Heritage Center in Park Hill, Oklahoma. The Cherokee Nation of Oklahoma was re-formed in 1970, and support for the Heritage Center became a line item in the tribal budget; it thus became eligible for tribal subsidies according to Mary Ellen Meredith, the interim director of the Cherokee Heritage Center, whom I interviewed in 1999. The Eastern Band's Museum of the Cherokee Indian became a tribally subsidized operation at approximately the same time (Finger 1993:155). The Cherokee historical organizations that allowed for the development of these museums insisted on extensive Indian participation. They hired increasing numbers of Cherokees into staff positions, and meetings were held at which Cherokees were allowed—indeed, encouraged—to voice their opinions on museum direction and development (King 1988:6).

An examination of some exhibition paradigms is useful at this point and will allow us to better discuss the direction and development of these Cherokee museums. Tribal entities quickly identified two directions they could pursue in constructing their tribal museums. The first was to develop exhibits that would be interesting to tourists at large while still promoting tribal perspectives. The other was to develop exhibits that would display tribal culture in such a way as to stimulate awareness and an ethic of preservation among tribal members (King 1988:4–5, a point reinforced by Meredith in our interview). The pros and cons of these two approaches have been the subject of debate for many tribal entities, as it certainly was for the Cherokees of North Carolina and Oklahoma. In both cases, a compromise position was the agreed course of action, although in practice the former position has won out over the latter. The biases of American archaeologists were retained at both localities because doing so was said to be giving the public at large what it wanted; it was to the financial advantage of the Cherokees to comply. The two Cherokee museums focused until the late 1990s on archaeological objects displayed with text that portrayed the Cherokee people in historical context. Lip service was given to ideas of cultural preservation, and from time to time ongoing archival projects would receive support. Concerns about cultural preservation were often listed in mission statements, but they frequently took a back seat to concerns about financial stability.

When the Tennessee Valley Authority (TVA) proposed to create the Tellico Reservoir, a heated debate took place, leading to results that have been disturbing to several constituencies in the area. The TVA largely ignored the individual rights of local residents, the impact on endangered species, and the concerns of the Cherokee people about the preservation of some of the most extensive archaeological remains in the Southeast. When the floodgates were closed on Tellico Lake in 1980, the remains of the Cherokee Overhill towns, the most important area of habitation in the eighteenth century, were inundated and now lie covered by water. There were extensive archaeological excavations of the Tellico site in the late 1960s and early 1970s, and in an attempt to placate the angry Cherokees, the Sequoyah Birthplace Museum was created on the shores of Tellico Lake in 1986 (King and Chapman 1993). This museum focused on general archaeology, the Overhill Cherokee, and the life and times of Sequoyah, the creator of the Cherokee syllabary, but like the other Cherokee museums its exhibits reflected standard archaeological perspectives.

The first Cherokee director of the Museum of the Cherokee Indian was hired in the mid-1980s. The Cherokee Heritage Center and the Sequoyah Birthplace Museum did not hire their first Cherokee directors until the 1990s, according to people I interviewed in 1999. With these museums now under Cherokee direction, a new and eager cadre of tribal museum personnel sought new ways to examine, exhibit, and preserve their culture, and to involve more Cherokees directly in the process. They benefited from advances in the science of museology, and, after some years of soul-searching, the Cherokee Heritage Center and the Museum of the Cherokee Indian decided on new directions for their exhibits. In 1998 the Cherokee Heritage Center opened a new permanent exhibit entitled, "Deferring to Our Elders." It was unlike anything ever before displayed at the museum; indeed, Meredith told me that the Heritage Center returned all the old display artifacts to TVA. This new, highly visual exhibit displays oversized photo images of contemporary Cherokee traditionalists participating in traditional lifeways. In addition, there is large, boldfaced print with quotes from respected elders and descriptions of traditional activities. Completing this sensory experience is an array of music and sound that changes from area to area within the exhibit. Such sensory bombardment is no longer uncommon in many types of museums, but it was a bold step for the Heritage Center since tribal museums have tended to shy away from such innovations (Lurie 1981:184).

After a $3.5 million renovation, the Museum of the Cherokee Indian incorporated new techniques inspired by the Heritage Center experiment, but they decided against giving away all their artifacts. As a compromise, the staff trimmed the total number of artifacts to be displayed by 80 percent; those that remained were presented to the public in a high-tech, richly visual manner. Lurie (1981:184) states that "museum exhibits, if done right, can have the visual impact of documentary film without the disadvantages of its ephemeral nature." In this spirit, the new museum features state-of-the-art video, fiber-optic lighting, extensive use of dioramas, and varied temperature-controlled environments to overwhelm the senses and emotions of visitors. Some criticize this "Disney-fied" exhibit style as too interpretive, but Lurie (1981:184) defends it, exclaiming, "if only we could pull in the Disney crowds to exhibits that might, for example, combat ethnocentrism compellingly and responsibly!" Perhaps in some small way, Lurie's seemingly over-optimistic statement has been realized as the changes at these two museums have been heralded as great successes, with many visitors giving glowing reviews.

Coincident with these changes in exhibit practice have come changes in mission statements for these museums. The new emphasis is on cultural preservation. Archival projects, especially those focusing on language preservation, have become common at both museums, according to Meredith and to Bo Taylor, the archivist at the Museum of the Cherokee Indian, whom I also interviewed in 1999. Moreover, these two museums constantly search for those within the Cherokee community who could aid in these endeavors. In recent years the museums have become venues for the demonstration of contemporary Cherokee life, and Cherokee musicians, craftspeople, and performers are found regularly interacting with the public.

Renovation of the Sequoyah Birthplace Museum is currently the subject of earnest discussion, although no timetable has yet been established by the Board of Directors. It should be noted that interested Cherokee individuals in the vicinity of Robbinsville, North Carolina, have recently opened the tribally subsidized Junaluska Museum, which, while still in its infancy, nonetheless demonstrates the Cherokee desire to preserve and share the cultural heritage.

At this point enlightened anthropologists and archaeologists may wonder what the next trend in Cherokee museology might be, and may be concerned about their own roles in future projects. I am myself a Cherokee tribal member and offer the following responses to these concerns, although I do so with the caution that there is really no widespread consensus among the Cherokee on these matters. Nevertheless, as director of the Sequoyah Birthplace Museum, I have visited with many Cherokees in trying to ascertain how the people wish their cultural heritage to be displayed. I have discussed with numerous Cherokee people what they expect from their centers of cultural heritage, what they would like to see these places do—and what they would want them never to do—and what they believe to be acceptable for a tribal museum to display or discuss. There has been startling diversity in the responses, but several trends seem to be emerging.

For example, in 1998 the Frank H. McClung Museum at the University of Tennessee in Knoxville began renovations on the Native Americans in Tennessee exhibit. The museum staff was very concerned about the Native American Graves Protection and Repatriation Act (NAGPRA) and its implication for displays of burial objects, funerary remains, or illustrations of excavated burials. Displaying great wisdom, the staff consulted with a number of tribal entities in an attempt to ascertain what would and would not be acceptable. The planning staff had already determined not to show photographs of burial exhumations, but they were surprised at how little resistance to their overall exhibit plan came from the Native Americans. With the exception of one person, most Cherokees were very impressed by the plans and did not object to the display of funerary objects. One tribal member pointed out that the nicest objects are usually found at funeral sites. Other museums in Tennessee have likewise consulted with local Native American groups, but there was perhaps surprisingly little resistance to the display of burials, photos of burials, and artifacts from burial sites. I myself have never heard a Cherokee voice such objections.

Cherokees certainly wish to respect their ancestors and protect their remains, but these goals do not come to the forefront in discussions about museums. Even when I explicitly brought up the subject, I was told that other matters were of more immediate concern. Taylor, for example, told me that the things he did not want to see at Cherokee museums were displays of the medicine aspects of Cherokee culture. As a traditionalist, he believes that this information should be preserved by Cherokees for Cherokees, and that displays of the associated ceremonialism should not be made available to the general public. This statement was repeated by Meredith, who felt that one "no no" for a Cherokee cultural center was to display and discuss medicine issues. The concern about medicine seemed to be a strong theme in the concerns voiced by those with whom I discussed the matter.

The people I spoke with also seemed to want to de-emphasize the Trail of Tears. I was surprised at this response, since a national Trail of Tears Historical Trail is in the final stages of development. Nevertheless, many Cherokees seem to think that there is too much attention given to this one event in Cherokee history. No one doubts its historical significance, but many feel that the Cherokees have made such progress since 1838–39 that all the discussion of the Trail of Tears tends to cast the Cherokee in the public image as victims and not as the proud people they are today.

Meredith also discussed the archaeological perspective. She has become aware of a profound resistance by many Cherokees to what white people consider archaeological "facts." She feels strongly that Cherokee museums should not feel compelled to portray current archaeological theories to the public. On the contrary, she thinks that a Cherokee museum should portray to the public a distinctly Cherokee view of the world and its history, for if such a portrayal is not presented by a Cherokee museum, it will not be done at all.

Finally, when I talked to Cherokees about what they most wanted to see at their museums, the most common answer was a desire to see the Cherokees portrayed as a living people with a dynamic culture that exists in many different places in the United States today. Taylor, for example, is heavily invested in this project and is currently working with Cherokee elders to produce a language program that would allow any interested party to become conversant in Cherokee. This program is based on a video–cd-rom interface that capitalizes on people's audio-visual learning capabilities. This program will not rely on print as a crutch. The Cherokee Heritage Center in Oklahoma also fosters language programs but considers its greatest strength to be as a venue for tribal elders to interact with the general public on an intimate basis. Mary Ellen Meredith believes that in this way the Heritage Center will meet its stated mission, to become "the world's best tribal education center for everybody."

REFERENCES

Alexander, Edward P. 1993. *Museums in Motion: An Introduction to the History and Functions of Museums*. Nashville: American Association for State and Local History.

Center for Museum Studies. 1998. *The Tribal Museum Directory*. Washington, D.C.: Smithsonian Institution.

Finger, John R. 1993. *Cherokee Americans: The Eastern Band of Cherokees in the Twentieth Century*. Lincoln: University of Nebraska Press.

King, Duane H., ed. 1988. *Cherokee Heritage: Official Guidebook to the Museum of the Cherokee Indian*. Cherokee, N.C.: Cherokee Communications.

King, Duane H., and Jefferson Chapman. 1993. *Official Guidebook to the Sequoyah Birthplace Museum*. Venore, Tenn.: Sequoyah Birthplace Museum.

Kuper, Adam. 1988. *The Invention of Primitive Society*. London: Routledge.

Lurie, Nancy O. 1981. Museumland Revisited. *Human Organization* 40 (2):181–87.

The Gendering of *Langue* and *Parole*: Literacy in Cherokee

Margaret C. Bender

The scholarship of the last generation has shown literacy to be a highly complex and diverse phenomenon, associated with a variety of practices, institutions, and ideologies in the specific cultural and historical contexts in which it has existed (Scribner and Cole 1981; Street 1984, 1993; Walker 1969, 1984). There are often gendered implications to the institutionalization and usage patterns of reading and writing in a given context. In this paper, I draw on interviews and participant observation carried out from 1993 to 1995 among the Eastern Band of Cherokee Indians to explore the question of whether there are gendered forms of literacy for these people. My interviews were conducted with adult users of the syllabary, and participant observation took place in Cherokee language classrooms for children and adults, in churches, at local social events, and through the day-to-day operations of a Cherokee language maintenance project with which I became involved. Most specifically, this paper discusses contemporary literacy in the Cherokee syllabary. Do Cherokee men read, write, collect, or use Cherokee language texts in ways that differ from those of Cherokee women? Do they express different beliefs about or attitudes toward literacy? And if they exist, what characterizes these differences and what can they tell us about related ways in which Cherokee life is and has been organized by gender? I hope that a focused study of practices and institutions related to literacy will contribute a new perspective to the diverse and growing literature on gender in Cherokee culture (e.g., Fogelson 1977, 1990; Hill 1997; Perdue 1995, 1998; Sattler 1995).

Cherokee has a particularly fascinating and rich history of literacy. The Cherokee syllabary was invented in the 1820s by a monolingual

Cherokee named Sequoyah (Holmes and Smith 1976). Although there were other scripts for Cherokee available at the time, Sequoyah's system was preferred and ultimately adopted by the Cherokee Nation government and people. By most accounts, the introduction of the system to the community was a great success, and the majority of the population quickly became literate. The syllabary was used in printings of the complete translated New Testament, some portions of the Old Testament, and other Christian texts. Government documents, such as the Cherokee Nation constitution, were printed using the new system, and the *Cherokee Phoenix*, a weekly bilingual newspaper, made use of it as well. Individuals reportedly used it for such purposes as personal and business correspondence, taking minutes, and recording medicine. Use of the syllabary continued after the removal of the Cherokee Nation to Indian Territory, and indeed its use continues among both Eastern and Western Cherokees today. The association of the syllabary with native Cherokee creativity and accomplishment, with religion, medicine, and the political and social infrastructure of the Nation, is fully reflected in today's use of and beliefs about the syllabary. What is perhaps more surprising is that these patterns of usage and belief seem to be interwoven with gendered patterns of work, representation, and communication.

GENDERED LITERACIES

Contemporary literacy in Cherokee plays a role in language education, tourism, religious and political practice, and the community's internal and external self-representations in ways that differentially affect the genders. The artistic objects conventionally produced by women (pottery, finger-woven belts, baskets) are much more likely than men's craft work to feature abstract designs, including syllabary characters (used, that is, as design elements, not as representations of the spoken language). I have also seen Cherokee women, but not men, offer to write visitors' names in syllabic characters, on something permanent like a small piece of wood; this is a somewhat more communicative or linguistically productive use of the system. By contrast, artistic commodities produced by men (e.g., wood carvings, ball sticks, and blow guns) do not generally feature abstract designs, nor are they marked with figures from the syllabary.

Some craft items are produced not for sale to tourists but for self-representation at community events like the annual Fall Festival. At this event, each of the seven Cherokee sub-communities prepares a display celebrating its agricultural, culinary, and artistic talents. Syllabic writing is often used in these presentations, and the one making the greatest use of the syllabary often seems to win the award for best display. One strategy for emphasizing the community's Cherokee language maintenance is to label the items in a display with characters from the syllabary; another is to include a syllabary chart, well worn Cherokee New Testament, and/or Cherokee hymnal in the display. But I have also seen the syllabary worked in very creatively, as on a needlepoint that won a blue ribbon one year. The most innovative project I saw was a large basket full of variously colored beans that had been grown in the community. The beans were arranged to spell out *Tsalaki* (Cherokee). Both of these pieces were identified as the work of women.

In language education, the semiotic division of labor is more complex and interesting. All three of the women teachers I knew in the mid-1990s used the syllabary in the classroom, whereas only half of the men (three out of six) did so. Even those men teachers who used syllabary texts in class generally did not write on the board or produce new texts using the syllabary, whereas women teachers did both. This tendency for women to be the classroom demonstrators of syllabic writing is consistent with their greater use of the syllabary for the artistic design of commodities. In fact, the syllabary is frequently used as a design to decorate classrooms and hallways, in student activities like coloring, and on tee shirts given to students as rewards—all examples of a similar educational mobilization of the syllabary.

In the mid-1990s, there were four orthographies for Cherokee, including the syllabary, that were used in language education as well as other contexts (see Holmes and Smith 1976 for examples). While children were visually exposed to the syllabary from the beginning of their school years, they were also taught a conventional way of writing Cherokee that was described by teachers as "phonetic," in which system the consonants have values roughly equivalent to those in English but the vowels have values (sometimes referred to as the "continental values") that must be learned. In this system, <a> stands for /a/, <e> for /e/, and so on. This system, which I refer to as the "standard phonetics," is reflected in the phonetic values on the syllabary chart, still in use today, that was popularized by Samuel Worcester in the pages of the *Cherokee Phoenix* in 1828. This system may also be considered "standard" because, as with the syllabary itself, spellings do not change to reflect the speaker's local dialect; it is understood that a standard phonetic spelling may be pronounced in various ways depending on the speaker's dialect and the context in which it occurs.

In the schools on the reservation, which most Cherokee children attend, children were expected to learn to read and write in this "phonetic" system beginning in the early grades, whereas they are not expected to start working regularly with the syllabary until the fourth grade.

The process of integrating the teaching of syllabary and standard phonetics was complicated by the fact that the teachers themselves displayed varying abilities and preferences with respect to the two systems. Some teachers used a third system, which I call "folk phonetics," in which <ah> might stand for /a/, other vowels might be written <ay>, <ee>, <oe>, <oo>, <uh>, and the writing of some consonants is altered to reflect dialectical pronunciations. Teachers advised the children to look at these spellings if they could not understand the standard phonetic system. One teacher called this system the "real" phonetics, explaining that students might, by reading these spellings, be able to "see a little bit better" how the words are pronounced. But this system works not because it is easy or genuine in some absolute sense but because its spellings rest firmly on the presupposed English language fluency and literacy of the students. The folk phonetic system was thus implicitly or explicitly identified as being closer to English and at the same time more accessible, more transparent, than other ways of writing Cherokee. On the other hand, the standard phonetic system, which is linked with the syllabary, was seen as more Cherokee (or, at least, less English) and also less accessible, at least to nonspeakers of Cherokee.

Yet another system of phonetic writing, one that closely resembles the systems generally used by linguists to write other Iroquoian languages, occasionally made its way into the classrooms. This system, preferred by at least one teacher, differs from the standard phonetic system in its writing of some consonants. Moreover, the glottal stop, vowel length, pitch, and intrusive *h*, all omitted from the standard phonetic writing, are recorded in this fourth system. The main spokesperson for the Eastern Cherokee Language Project worked extensively in the 1970s with a linguist, developing in the process quite a bit of material on this system for use by classroom teachers. Because of its local associations, I refer to this system as "high phonetics," which, although clearly intended as a relatively more narrow means of transcription than either the syllabary or the other two phonetic systems, was seen by many as being difficult and inaccessible—not unlike the syllabary itself. In particular, language teachers complained (or reported that their students complained) about the use of <k> and <t> for /k/ and /t/. One teacher particularly objected to the use of <th> to represent /th/. <th>, he told me, stands for the first sounds in "this, that, and Thatcher!" "He considered the use of <kw> and <khw> as contrasted with the <qu> spellings on the syllabary chart to be "wrong" as well. I have heard this objection from other speakers, and wonder whether <q> might be preferred because it resembles a <g> and thus is considered to stand easily for both the aspirated and unaspirated versions of the consonant.

The presence of these four writing systems, and the perceived need for teachers and students to move among them, suggested a range of accessibility to would-be readers and writers of Cherokee, with folk phonetics being the most accessible (to readers of English) and the syllabary being least accessible. This hierarchy obscured the fact that the syllabary is, by definition, a phonetic writing system, although it is, to be sure, a system for relatively broad transcription. The presence of folk phonetics implies that even the standard phonetic system is not easily memorized and does not come easily to readers and writers of English.

The syllabary emerged from this culturally specific pattern of distribution with a very special set of associations: it was treated in formal language education as inaccessible and essentially nonphonetic. Indeed, it was treated more like a code that might be substituted for phonetic scripts than like a phonetic script itself. Several aspects of its usage further reinforced the code-like nature of the system. For example, students almost never memorized the syllabary but transliterated in and out of it with the assistance of the omnipresent chart, which functioned as a sort of key. Students and teachers both tended to copy the shapes of characters exactly as they appeared on the chart; the characters' shapes were emphasized in other ways not characteristic of the letters in phonetic scripts. The use of the syllabary by students tended to be nonproductive, in that new texts were rarely produced in it. But while the syllabary seemed in these ways to be distanced from the spoken language, its close relationship to Cherokee culture was reinforced. The syllabary was never used, for example, for English-language punning; its phonemic values were never appropriated for use outside of Cherokee. The syllabary was also most likely to appear in classroom use when the lesson content was specifically Cherokee in nature (e.g., a lesson on the colors associated in Cherokee with the four cardinal directions). In adult education, these cultural associations extended to Cherokee Christianity. The syllabary also assumed a more generalized positive value via its role in language education. Other Cherokee orthographies, like written English, were treated as systems children would not inherently want to use or enjoy using. Indeed, nonsyllabic Cherokee writing and English-language writing were both assigned to students, especially in the middle and high schools, as punishments. By contrast, reading and writing in syllabary often takes the form of an extra-credit or special-event activity.

These patterns of usage convey important messages about the syllabary. First, the syllabary is strongly linked with the Cherokee community and is not for general use. Second, the syllabary is hard to use, and its use is therefore reserved for mature specialists, who tend to be active Christians, language and culture experts, or medicine men and women.

In Cherokee language classrooms, the four orthographic systems serve different functions and carry different implicit messages. "High phonetics" indexes one's membership in a fairly elite group and one's status as a linguistic expert. Both the syllabary and the standard phonetic system (which usually appear together on the conventional chart) index one's faithfulness to a traditionally Cherokee way of writing, although the syllabary is much more specifically associated with Cherokee cultural content and contexts. The folk phonetic system expresses a kind of orthographic populism, a way to reach out to those whose first language is not Cherokee.

It is interesting, then, to note that the folk phonetic system seems to characterize a primarily male orthographic space. All the language teachers I encountered who used this system in educational settings were men. Indeed, all of the Cherokees I met who were active users of folk phonetics were men. Evidence of this pattern could be found beyond the classroom in the community's semiotic landscape as well. For example, one male language teacher who also taught Sunday school used folk phonetics to post the first verse of "Amazing Grace" in Cherokee on his church's announcement board and in the church bulletin. The names of fallen soldiers, written on the Cherokee Veterans Memorial, arguably a male-focused space, constituted the only other public display of folk phonetics.

One of the only products to make use of folk phonetics in the field of tourism was a book by two male authors and seemingly oriented toward a male readership: *How to Talk Trash in Cherokee*. I have always been struck by the fact that this book contains material otherwise absent from the self-representations that constitute Cherokee cultural tourism. It addresses topics such as meeting women, drinking, and "talking trash" as the title suggests. I was thus very surprised to learn, from a conservative, middle-aged woman social worker, that she and other Cherokees enjoyed the book and even found it hilarious. But later I realized that the production, distribution, and consumption of this book could be seen as constituting a kind of late-twentieth-century textual booger dance, a traditional form in which caricatures of inappropriately behaving outsiders are acted out (Fogelson and Walker 1980; Speck and Broom 1951). This variation on the booger dance is particularly comical, since it is presumably consumed by white tourists under the mistaken impression that they are learning about something truly Cherokee—the book, after all, is in the Cherokee language!—while they are actually seeing a textual critique of their own behavior. I do not believe that it is coincidental that this book is written in folk phonetics (which is, as noted above, also a system of Anglicized phonetics) and not just because of the purported tourist audience. This crude and explicit content would not be at all appropriate to communicate via the code of the syllabary.

Cherokee men seem to be associated with folk phonetics in public spaces, although they certainly do not only use this system. Men are more likely than women to be Sunday school teachers, which means that they are authoritative readers of the syllabary and that they teach others to read it aloud. Men are also likely to possess notebooks that contain the syllabic medicinal texts discussed by Walker in his article in this volume. Women who told me of medicinal notebooks in their families generally described them as having belonged to a father or an uncle, although they sometimes described having been responsible for the transfer of a notebook from one male relative to another. I was also sometimes told of personal journals that were kept in syllabic writing by men but not by women.

HOW AND WHY MEN AND WOMEN HAVE
LEARNED THE SYLLABARY

Among the Cherokee I interviewed who were literate in the syllabary, women were much more likely to have learned the system in the context and for the purposes of formal language education (four out of ten vs. one out of eight). Some of the women did not identify a desire to teach Cherokee in the formal sense as their motive for learning the syllabary; they instead cited their love of the language and/or their desire to expose others to it in some informal fashion. One such woman was a potter and former kindergarten teacher. She neither read nor wrote (in the sense of productively transcribing spoken language), but she could reproduce the syllabary on paper or clay by heart. She said that the syllabary was "embedded in [my] mind like on [my] pottery."

The syllabary, like the ancient designs we see in museums, will be "embedded in the clay" of her pottery, preserved like stories she was told in childhood and that are now preserved in her memory. Her hope, she said, was that in the future people will know that the Cherokee people had a written language, just as we now have access to knowledge about ancient peoples from their pottery. This woman was clearly motivated by the need for preservation, but the implication was that her preserved writing would be mute in the future. She did not suggest that in the future people would be able to "read" her pottery; the script on them is not meaningful in that sense. But the existence of the characters on her pottery will point toward the history of a system of meaningful writing, and that conceptual history is what she seeks to preserve.

Men, by contrast, tended to be motivated to learn the syllabary by a desire to grow in faith or Biblical knowledge. (Women who talked about faith as a motive almost always did so in combination with the educational objectives noted above.) There also seemed to be something of a difference in the place of syllabary learning in the life cycles of men and women. The modal age for Cherokee women to have learned the syllabary was thirty, with very little deviation, but men learned the syllabary anywhere from early childhood to age forty-one. In addition to sometimes learning the syllabary at a younger age, men were more likely to have been taught by a relative, usually a male such as a grandfather, father, or uncle. No women seem to have been taught by a relative.

IMPLICATIONS

It seems generally the case that women are more likely to use the syllabary in public contexts, while men are more likely to be the primary users of the syllabary in contexts that are relatively private (e.g., churches and homes that are relatively free of unwanted non-Cherokee outsiders) or *very* private (e.g., medicinal practice). While women mobilized the syllabary in public, they did not generally use it in the communicative sense; indeed, the role it serves in language education perpetuates a kind of barrier to its widespread usage.

I believe that two interpretations of these patterns can be ruled out. One cannot understand the apparent responsibility of women for the public presentation of the syllabary and men's monopoly on folk phonetics in the public realm as simply a gendered division along the lines of sacred vs. profane, nor along the lines of the traditional Cherokee vs. Anglo orientation. There is a kind of inversion between the public and private uses of these writing systems, so that both men and women are associated with the spiritual and with Cherokee culture, through reading and/or writing, in different contexts. Moreover, I do not think one could summarize this case as one in which men exclusively control meaningful access to and use of literacy in its most powerful local contexts—the religious and medicinal—while women are denied access to the power of literacy. Public self-representation of the community and formal education are two extremely important local arenas, and women's control of the mobilization of the syllabary in these contexts should not be undervalued.

Three alternative ways of thinking about these gendered patterns seem plausible. First, it seems possible that Cherokee women, in their public usage of the syllabary, are acting in the role of cultural mediators (Kidwell 1992), who transmit a community's image and select knowledge to outsiders and to youth and simultaneously control access to the community's more protected knowledge. A second, related way of looking at this pattern would suggest that there is a kind of gender role reversal between public and private contexts that helps to protect the community's precious core of knowledge, belief, and practice from outsiders and the immature. Women are public mobilizers of the syllabary, then, specifically because men are more likely to be the private users of the system. The following anecdote, told to me in the mid-1990s by one of the very few Cherokees under the age of thirty who was literate in the syllabary (taught by his grandfather), is suggestive:

Yeah, it was, I guess, about when I was age thirteen. I was sitting on the porch with my grandfather, and he was already pretty sick and he just one day just started talking about the Cherokee alphabet, and how it was used and things. Well, he just—just took out a carpenter's pencil and then a brown paper bag, a brown shopping bag, started writing down the symbols that he could remember, and their sounds. And he was teaching me at that time how, you know, that you put 'em together, what they say. . . . I guess we got about to row four on the alphabet when he just couldn't—he couldn't go any further, he couldn't remember. After he died, I never thought about what he had told me about the alphabet and stuff, you know; it just brought back bad memories.

About two years later he went back to the syllabary, and completed teaching himself how to read and write. But his efforts were not met with universal approval:

I was at one time accused—oh, I just hate to use that word—I guess [of] witchcraft. Being so young, and knowing that . . . someone had made a statement to one of my relatives that, someone's training him, or someone's teaching him, because they said that there's no other reason why a person should know that at a young age. Then I thought, well, I better be reserved with this as to how I use it and stuff because people will get—people will get that impression, you know, 'cause it was in my family at one time, the older people in my family, they were known for that. They—I guess they were just under the assumption that that's what it was for. I learned it 'cause I wanted—'cause my grandpa wanted me to.

The community's attitude led this boy at least to alter or conceal his reading and writing practices. Perhaps a heavier burden of interpretation placed on public syllabary-related activities on the part of men is in part responsible for women's greater public use of the syllabary.

Finally, I think it may help to consider women's public uses of the syllabary as providing the necessary infrastructure for continued syllabic literacy. Women are keeping the system alive through art, through useful products and commodities, and through the knowledge imparted to children that the system exists and is ready for their mastery and use when the time is right. The maintenance of such a system and its execution are mutually interdependent, and it is impossible to prioritize them. An extremely profound complementarity is thus revealed in the symbolic and communicative division of labor between Cherokee men and women.

NOTE

I gratefully acknowledge the financial support provided by the American Philosophical Society and the Spencer Foundation for my 1993–95 fieldwork with the Eastern Band of Cherokee Indians.

REFERENCES

Fogelson, Raymond D. 1977. Cherokee Notions of Power. In *The Anthropology of Power: Ethnographic Studies from Asia, Oceania, and the New World*, ed. Raymond D. Fogelson and Richard N. Adams. 185–94. New York: Academic Press.

———. 1990. On the "Petticoat Government" of the Eighteenth-Century Cherokee. In *Personality and the Cultural Construction of Society*, ed. David K. Jordan and Marc J. Swartz. 161–81. Tuscaloosa: University of Alabama Press.

Fogelson, Raymond D., and Amelia B. Walker. 1980. Self and Other in Cherokee Booger Masks. *Journal of Cherokee Studies* 5(2):88–102.

Hill, Sarah. 1997. *Weaving New Worlds: Southeastern Cherokee Women and Their Basketry*. Chapel Hill: University of North Carolina Press.

Holmes, Ruth Bradley, and Betty Sharp Smith. 1976. *Beginning Cherokee*. Norman: University of Oklahoma Press.

Kidwell, Clara Sue. 1992. Indian Women as Cultural Mediators. *Ethnohistory* 39(2):97–107.

Perdue, Theda. 1995. Women, Men and American Indian Policy: The Cherokee Response to "Civilization." In *Negotiators of Change: Historical Perspectives on Native American Women*, ed. Nancy Shoemaker. 90–114. New York: Routledge.

———. 1998. *Cherokee Women: Gender and Culture Change, 1700–1835*. Lincoln: University of Nebraska Press.

Sattler, Richard A. 1995. Women's Status among the Muskogee and Cherokee. In *Women and Power in Native North America*, ed. Laura F. Klein and Lillian A. Ackerman. 214–29. Norman: University of Oklahoma Press.

Scribner, Sylvia, and Michael Cole. 1981. *The Psychology of Literacy*. Cambridge, Mass.: Harvard University Press.

Speck, Frank G., and Leonard Broom (in collaboration with Will West Long). 1951. *Cherokee Dance and Drama*. Berkeley: University of California Press.

Street, Brian V. 1984. *Literacy in Theory and Practice*. Cambridge, U.K.: Cambridge University Press.

————. 1993. *Cross-Cultural Approaches to Literacy*. Cambridge, U.K.: Cambridge University Press.

Walker, Willard. 1969. Notes on Native Writing Systems and the Design of Native Literacy Programs. *Anthropological Linguistics* 11(5):148–66.

————. 1984. Literacy, Wampums, the Gudebuk, and How Indians in the Far Northeast Read. *Anthropological Linguistics* 26(1):42–52.

Gender Reciprocity and Ritual Speech among the Yuchi

Jason Baird Jackson

Sometime around 1884, an unknown Yuchi narrator related to Jeremiah Curtin a tale of "the first woman who wouldn't live with a lazy husband." The story is found in Curtin's unpublished notes, which are filed in the National Anthropological Archives at the National Museum of Natural History (Smithsonian Institution):

> A long time ago there was a man and a pigeon. The pigeon married the man's sister and after the pigeon was married he went off into the field to work but he sat on the stump of a dead tree cooing. The woman cooked dinner and went out into the field to call her husband [and] found him sitting on the tree cooing. He went to the house with her. He wasn't good to work and at last the woman left him. Her next husband was a mocking bird. He went into the field to work too. The woman got dinner and went to call him [but] she found him singing all sorts of songs. He hadn't done a bit of work. He went home to dinner and stayed all day and all night, but she found he wasn't a worker and she turned him off. Her third husband was a lizard. He went into the field [and] she heard no noise at all. At noon she went to call him [and] found him hard at work, cutting down every blade of grass. He was a good worker and the woman was satisfied. They lived happily. This was the first woman who wouldn't live with a lazy husband.

This brief story encapsulates ideas Yuchi people continue to hold about the qualities that characterize worthy men and women. It also illustrates the powers of choice that Yuchi women have long possessed, and the divisions of labor that Yuchi people associate with gender. In this essay, I will explore such issues as they play out in Yuchi society today.

YUCHI CULTURE

Before examining ritual, ritual speech, and gender more specifically, those unfamiliar with the general situation of the Yuchi and other woodland native peoples in Oklahoma may benefit from some preliminary comments on Yuchi language, culture, and society. The Yuchi have lived in eastern Oklahoma since the 1830s, arriving in what was then known as Indian Territory in the company of Muskogee (Creek) peoples, among whom they had maintained their own autonomous towns prior to being forcibly removed from their territories east of the Mississippi River by the U.S. government. After removal, the Yuchi reestablished their own communities in the northwest corner of the Creek Nation, near the present-day municipalities of Bixby, Sapulpa, and Bristow, Oklahoma. The Yuchi language is unrelated to Creek, and the Yuchi constitute the most culturally divergent minority population politically encompassed within the modern, multiethnic Muskogee (Creek) Nation. Population estimates are difficult to assemble, but during the nineteenth and twentieth centuries the Yuchi seem to have consistently comprised about 15 percent of the total Creek Nation population. Today, knowledgeable Yuchi people estimate the tribal population at between 1,500 and 2,000 individuals.

Yuchi culture is broadly similar to that of other native horticultural groups whose histories are rooted in the woodlands of eastern North America. Despite their political encapsulation within the Muskogee (Creek) Nation, the Yuchi preserve many distinctive social and cultural traditions that set them apart from their Creek neighbors. In particular, the Yuchi maintain close ties with the Absentee Shawnee. Yuchi culture patterns are shared as much with the Shawnee and other northeastern groups as with the Creek and other peoples speaking Muskogean languages. Speck (1909) and Jackson (1998a, 1998b) provide general descriptions of Yuchi culture and society.

Lacking federal recognition as a distinct tribe, the Yuchi rely on older community institutions, particularly three town-based ceremonial grounds and two Methodist church congregations, to help organize their society. Language and cultural preservation activities have become important foci of Yuchi community life, expanding a longstanding seasonal round of secular and sacred activities. The three ceremonial grounds continue to be the most prominent institutions of Yuchi social life. While functioning as religious congregations today, the ceremonial grounds are, in form and historical origin, town governments en-compassing the secular and religious life of a local Yuchi settlement pos-sessing a town square, the physical form providing the ceremonial ground with its English-language label. In contrast to nineteenth-century practice, not all Yuchi people today participate in ceremonial ground life, although many do so. Despite attrition via assimilation to Euro-American social life, the ceremonial grounds are today still the social foci and cultural symbols of local Yuchi communities. They retain the town-square architecture they have possessed since time immemor-ial, and they continue to be led by a town chief, one or more assistant chiefs, a speaker, and a committee of chief's advisors. These men orga-nize a series of ceremonial events that take place at each settlement's ground site, beginning with ritual football games in early spring and con-tinuing through an event known as the Soup Dance in the late summer or early fall. During the winter season the ceremonial ground organiza-tions are ritually inactive, but they continue to organize secular social activities for the Yuchi community, including holiday dinners, wild onion suppers, and indoor "just for fun" dances. This seasonal round is described in Jackson (1998b).

Elsewhere (Jackson 1996, 1998a) I have described Yuchi ceremonial ground oratory in general terms without focusing on its interaction with ideas about gender. Here, I intend to use one oratory performance and its cultural setting to explore what such "talks" say, literally and figura-tively, about the place of men and women in Yuchi society. I acknowl-edge that reliance here on a man's speech about a woman's ritual pre-sents an incomplete account of a significant cultural performance. On the other hand, the value of a discourse-centered approach is that it takes the facts as found on the ground in real social events as a starting point for analysis. Certainly the gendered division of labor underlying this rit-ual is a fundamental part of the event and its context.

As Buckley (1989:305) notes, the Yuchi Ribbon Dance, which takes place within the annual multi-day Green Corn Ceremonial, is an espe-cially important instance in which ideas about gender are formalized and made public. This dance is one of the most important rituals in the sea-sonal round of Yuchi life. It entails the women of the local community dancing alone in the town square, the only Yuchi dance in which this practice is followed. While Buckley (1989) and Ballard (1978) offer complex structural analyses of this event within the larger frame of

Yuchi ceremonialism, neither presents a Yuchi exegesis, although such explication is a regular part of the event itself.

Of the three Yuchi ceremonial grounds, the Polecat community near Kellyville, Oklahoma, has preserved the fullest version of the Green Corn Ceremonial throughout the twentieth century. During the 1990s the Duck Creek community near Hectorville actively reestablished older Yuchi ceremonial practices that had been maintained by their Polecat relatives but which had been absent in the simpler version of the Green Corn Ceremonial they had maintained since their ceremonial ground was reactivated in the early 1940s. One such reintroduction took place on June 24, 1994, on which occasion the Yuchi Ribbon Dance was held in the Duck Creek town for the first time since the 1920s.

REVIEW OF LITERATURE

Anthropological studies of Yuchi language, culture, society, and history are relatively few, and the work that has been published has been more descriptive than analytical. One notable exception to this generalization is Buckley's (1989) interesting and theoretically rich study of Yuchi gender symmetry. Buckley drew on published and unpublished sources available in the 1970s to craft a model of gender relations in Yuchi culture. The semiotics of Yuchi expressive culture and social relations suggested to Buckley that a model of gender complementarity is a fundamental principle in Yuchi society. Such symbolic or semiotic studies of small-scale societies may seem to be of only academic interest to a small group of anthropologists, but the issue central to Buckley's analysis has a wider significance for understanding the variety of ways human societies have culturally constructed and socially enacted fundamental understandings of what it means to be male and female. As Yanagisako and Collier (1994) have pointed out, the cross-cultural study of local differences between men and women helps destabilize the biological folk wisdom of cosmopolitan European societies, upon which both contemporary social relations and anthropological studies of kinship and gender have foundered.

Since the early 1990s non-Yuchi scholars, as well as members of the Yuchi community itself, have greatly expanded the ethnographic, linguistic, and historical record bearing on the community and its past. Since 1993 I have worked closely with Yuchi people in a series of studies and projects focusing on Yuchi culture and language. I have resided in the Yuchi community since 1995 and have participated in its ceremonial activities continually since that date. My reading of Buckley's study is conditioned by my long-term commitment to Yuchi ethnography and by the enduring friendships I have made with Yuchi people. Recent Yuchi ethnography suggests that Buckley's argument is fundamentally correct but that the ethnography on which it was constructed is partial and subject to revision. These revisions in turn suggest useful modifications of Buckley's position. In light of this observation, and in substantiation thereof, this essay, together with others currently in preparation, will serve two purposes—to update the record of cultural, historical, linguistic, and social data on which Buckley's account rests while re-examining his hypothesis in light of the more abundant information presently available.[1]

The portion of this broader project that I will explore here reopens the study of Yuchi gender roles as seen through the window of publicly circulating ritual and civic discourse, an approach that follows from a discourse-centered perspective on culture, one that is current in much contemporary linguistic anthropology. This perspective is itself rooted more broadly in what has come to be known as the Americanist tradition (Bauman and Briggs 1990; Darnell 1999; Sherzer 1987; Urban 1991). The concerns I will explore here address old interests in American anthropology. Boas (1940) called for close study of oratory of all types, while his student Gladys Reichard authored a justly famous monograph, *Prayer: The Compulsive Word* (1944), which used ceremonial prayer as a starting point for a comprehensive study of religion in Navajo life.

AN ANALYSIS OF ORATORY AND CEREMONY

In June 1994, Esther Littlebear assumed the role of head dancer, a position she continues to fill to this day. Her brother-in-law, Newman Littlebear, served as the lead singer. Mr. Littlebear is the chief's speaker for the Polecat Ceremonial Ground and is one of that ground's dance singers. Assisting the Duck Creek chief and assistant chief in this new undertaking was Polecat Chief James Brown Sr. On this special occasion, the Duck Creek chief asked Mr. Littlebear to speak to the assembled ceremonial ground members and guests and to explain the significance of the dance. Mr. Littlebear has had a long career as a ceremonial ground orator, and his speech on this occasion was typical of those he regularly delivered during ceremonial ground events. It is similar, in particular, to those he has regularly delivered prior to performances of the Ribbon Dance in his home community. For my purposes, it first exemplifies the male ritual oratory genre Mr. Littlebear has successfully reconstituted after a community-wide shift from Yuchi- to English-language fluency. More specifically, Mr. Littlebear's talk on this occasion provides access to a publicly circulating discourse on gender in Yuchi society.

The text presented below is derived from a videotape recording of the event. I have explained the rationale behind my transcription format elsewhere (Jackson 1998a, 1998b) but note here that the breaks corresponding roughly to written sentences are signaled in performance by quite noticeable breath-marked pauses, while the line breaks correspond to shorter pauses in delivery.

An Oratory Delivered by Mr. Newman Littlebear Preceding the Revived Performance of the Ribbon Dance at the Duck Creek Ceremonial Ground During Its Annual Green Corn Ceremonial, Friday, June 24, 1994

(1) The leader
     of this ceremonial
     he asked me to say something about this—
     this Women's Dance
     or Ribbon Dance.
(2) I know many of us
     have saw these dances
     from year to year.
(3) But what I want to say a little bit
     of what our—
     what our elders
     before us
     before my time
     before
     any of us [said].
(4) That amongst our people
     our tribal people
     they had

       carried this out
       from year to year.
(5)   And if I asked somebody
       or you asked somebody:
          "What is a Ribbon Dance?"
          "What is it for?"
       we might have our own ideas and thoughts.
(6)   But according to the elders
       of our people
       they tell us
       that it's a—
       it's a high honor
       to be a part of this
       especially the ones
       that's going to perform
       for us this evening.
(7)   THEY SAY it's ah
       an honor.
(8)   It's about life.
(9)   It's about creation.
(10)   It's about
       the different colors
       in this universe.
(11)   The sky above.
(12)   The sun.
(13)   The moon.
(14)   The rain.
(15)   The vegetation.
(16)   All of creation.
(17)   Perhaps that
       head you see out there.
(18)   Different colors.
(19)   And our fire.
(20)   And even our—
       our colors
       the colors of people
       in the world
       in this creation.

(21)   And the colors that come from the mother earth.
(22)   All the vegetation
        from different times of the year.
(23)   You see many colors.
(24)   And also
        it—
        it has been said
        this is the way
        our mothers
        our daughters
        and grandchildren
        this is their way
        the ladies' way
        of honoring
        us men folks.
(25)   It's sacred.
(26)   This is their way
        that our people had
        to honor us men folks
        to perform for us.
(27)   To show
        the Almighty
        that we are proud
        of what—
        of his creation.
(28)   Like giving a thanks
        for all of us.
(29)   This is bestowed upon them.
(30)   That is why we say that this is
        a high honor
        for them to be part of this
        and we just wish them well
        in this dance
        this evening.
(31)   That they may enjoy.
(32)   That as they
        move about around
        the holy fire

that they will feel
an inspiration
from above.

(33)   This is what our elders tell us.

(34)   This is like the beginning of our ceremony here this weekend.

(35)   So.

(36)   Just bear with us
and we are going to try
to continue on.

(37)   Perhaps there are many other
things that could be said
that we can't say to you
that we don't know about—
about this ribbon dance.

(38)   But that's according to the ones
before us
[what they] have left for us.

(39)   They instructed us
to do this
as long as we possibly can.

(40)   And as the brother said
this is their first time here.

(41)   But
perhaps it is just the beginning.

(42)   I hear the people here say we have a lot of women folks
shell shakers
and you do have.

(43)   This is not all of them
you have many more yet
that are not out here to perform.

(44)   But perhaps
in the times to come
it will multiply.

(45)   So with that
we thank each and every one of you
for your attention.

(46)   Thank you.

(47)   [Men respond, loudly and in unison]: *hõ*.

The first passage in the text suggests a pattern that is repeated through-out the speech and others of its genre. What is generally referred to in linguistic anthropological analysis as "authorship" (Goffman 1981) is addressed when Mr. Littlebear notes that the speech has been sponsored by the ground's chief, whom speakers such as himself serve. Author-ship is also at issue when Mr. Littlebear refers to the speech of Yuchi ancestors whose words he is transmitting. As DuBois (1986) and Chafe (1993), among others, have noted, these uses of language distribute and transfer responsibility for public speech and provide it with a source of authority greater than the speaker her/himself. Referring in the second and third spoken units to the antiquity of the Ribbon Dance as a Yuchi ceremonial further enhances the authority of this speech; it also addresses members of the audience who are unfamiliar with it, due to its reintro-duced status in the Duck Creek community.

When Mr. Littlebear begins to provide an interpretation of the dance, he immediately opens up discussion of the three primary modes of rec-iprocal interaction and dependence characteristic of social relationships in Yuchi ceremony in particular and in Yuchi society as a whole. The first mode is the interactional interdependence and conceptual separation of men and women. Beginning with passage 6, he makes indirect reference to the special status of women as performers in the ritual, noting that their role is considered a special honor distinct to them. As he notes in passage 24, Yuchi women honor Yuchi men through performance of this dance. What is not said here but is regularly stated in discussions among male ceremonialists is that male conduct is especially important during this dance. During the vigorous sections of the dance, the men are expected to offer shouts of encouragement in the Yuchi language to the women. At the conclusion of each round of dancing, the men together intone the Yuchi word *hõ*, which signifies both "yes" (in the sense of "agreed") and "thank you." With this same remark, men collectively rat-ify a public speech, as in line 47. Younger Yuchi men are told explicitly that such attentive and respectful behavior is the means by which they honor the women of their family and town. In addition, certain men are selected to oversee and enact the musical and ritual practices that accompany the dancing of the women. This work also signals respect and support for the women of the local community.

Yuchi women are silent during the ceremonies that take place within the town's square ground, a pattern also reported by Bell (1990:333) as common among the Creek. The women dance while men speak and sing publicly. At the same time, the women provide the musical accompaniment for many ceremonial songs through the use of leg rattles that only they can wear. The Ribbon Dance reflects Yuchi society in a more general way. Men and women are separate classes of social beings, but these two classes are complementary and dependent on one another to complete the form and functioning of the social body. Nevertheless, to characterize the classes in this way is not the same as saying that they are "symmetrical," as Buckley's (1989:308–9) analysis might suggest. The Yuchi case of women and men is structurally parallel to the case of dual organization as analyzed by Lévi-Strauss (1944a, 1944b, 1963; for the dual organization of Yuchi men, see Jackson 1996). As suggested by Yanagisako and Collier's (1994:195–96) reassessment of gender and kinship studies and marking theory in linguistics, systems of reciprocity co-occur with a pattern of social hierarchy (see also Jakobson 1990). In the case of Yuchi gender relations, male activities, particularly community and ritual leadership, define the nature of the social fabric as a whole. Yuchi men control the public social order, but they do so with full knowledge that their role is partial and dependent on the special capabilities and tasks of their female social partners. Men are dominant in Yuchi public ritual life but, being powerful in important ways men lack, women are recognized as both distinct and essential to the life of society as a whole. Conversely, women are dominant in the domestic sphere but require the special contribution men make to this domain.

These patterns suggest a kind of cross-cultural continuum, at one end of which are those societies that can come close to an ideal of perfect reciprocity without hierarchy. For purposes of future discussion, I would suggest, based on my life experience in eastern Oklahoma, that one group allied to the Yuchi, the Shawnee, represent a case one step closer than the Yuchi to this ideal; their other allies, the Creek, are one step further removed. Sufficient ethnographic material exists to explore this question in greater detail. In addition to work on the Creek spanning the time of Swanton (1928) to that of Bell (1990), there are Voegelin's (1936) discussions of the Shawnee female deity and Howard's (1981) account of their "Queen Lady" and her ritual responsibilities.

Such patterns are mostly visible in social terms, but, to students of male and female symbolism in Native North American cultures, certain cultural ideas about gender and women that are expressed in Mr. Littlebear's speech, while not surprising, nonetheless illuminate Yuchi values and beliefs. Mother Earth, mentioned in line 21, is an obvious example, as is the reference in passage 24 to successive generations of women as characterized in their primary role as Yuchi mothers. Motherhood, domestic stability, and female generativity on one level are here linked and bundled symbolically with natural renewal and supernatural blessing. Fogelson (1990) has explored these linkages in greater detail in his studies of women's roles in Cherokee social organization and government.

Consideration of the association of the social and cosmological domains leads to discussion of two additional patterns of reciprocity in the Yuchi way of life. These two modes of social relations are, I argue, as significant as the patterns of gender reciprocity identified by Buckley, Bell, and others. In the sections that immediately follow the linking of women with the honor of Ribbon Dance performance, Mr. Littlebear addresses the dancers' participation in the wider framework of meaning attached to Yuchi communal ceremonialism in general. In this framework, the dance is an expression of Yuchi appreciation for the beauty and, most importantly, the productivity of earthly creation as manifest in the seasonal round of natural and ritual activity. While gender roles are made public in the Ribbon Dance and in Mr. Littlebear's speech, another relationship of interdependence and responsibility is also noted: that existing between the earthly Yuchi community on the one hand, and the Creator and Yuchi ancestors on the other. Thanksgiving, best known as a fundamental principle in Iroquois ceremonialism, is the theme at work here and elsewhere in Yuchi communal ritual. Following Yuchi public discourse, I have interpreted Yuchi ritual as a means of collective thanksgiving, but this same discourse also suggests that such ritual is also a collective responsibility. As in Iroquois ritual, these factors are two sides of the same coin. In the Ribbon Dance, Yuchi men and women honor and thank each other for their separate contributions to maintaining the social order, while for both men and women the dance is an opportunity to honor and thank the Creator for maintaining cosmological order.

In undertaking both these goals, the Yuchi communicate respect toward their own ancestors who, in their own time, fulfilled these ongoing obligations while teaching them to younger generations. Such generational reciprocity is the third dynamic theme at work in Yuchi social life. Mr. Littlebear makes repeated reference to ancestral performance of the dance and to inherited interpretations of it. As noted in passage 39, it is the obligation of the living to keep faith with their teachers and with Yuchi traditions as transmitted from generation to generation. As I have described elsewhere (Jackson 1998b), the spirits of departed Yuchi return to participate in community rituals. They are considered to be pleased when these activities continue to come up in the seasonal round. As various students of the cosmologies of Native people of the Southeast have noted, there is a flip side to reciprocal relations between constituent groups that is not often stated publicly but is well known among the Yuchi and their neighbors. To fail to carry on ancestral ritual in a proper and respectful manner leads to misfortune and poor health. The spirits of the dead play a sanctioning role in this matter as well, just as disharmony between humans and the Creator, or neglect of the duties that define relations between men and women, produce negative consequences.

SPEECH AND GENDER: SOME GENERAL CHARACTERISTICS

The Ribbon Dance illustrates in some obvious ways the theme of generational hierarchy and reciprocity. The line of women dancers is fixed. Throughout a woman's life, she moves forward in a line whose sequence is determined by seniority. The head woman is she who has participated for the longest time. The tail of the line is composed of young girls dancing for the first time. Maintaining proper order over the succession of years is one of the most passionately observed protocols in Yuchi ritualism. It is a manifestation of the fundamental Woodland Indian principle of age equating with knowledge, power, and respect (Fogelson 1977:187).

The Creator, through the gift of this special dance, honors women. With it they honor both their male relatives and creation. In ceding to women the performative role in square ground ritual, their male relatives communicate respect for and appreciation of women for their effort in this collective thanksgiving. By renewing this ceremonial for another year, Yuchis signal respect for their ancestors whose own efforts led to its continued existence in the Yuchi world. This respect creates harmonious relations between the living and the dead, a circumstance that generates the "holy" and "inspired" feeling that Mr. Littlebear describes in passage 32. In serving these ends, the living Yuchi also enact principles of social order in this world. These principles divide and organize society on the basis of gender but also in terms of age and patrilineal descent (as manifest in the division of Yuchi men into "chiefs" and "warriors").

The brief analysis of ritual oratory presented here reflects a static model of Yuchi social relations. Some sense of social change within this enduring model of social order and continuity can be seen through a condensed and anecdotal discussion of another genre of ritual speaking: prayer. On Saturday, April 27, 1996, the members of the Duck Creek Ceremonial round gathered for their fourth and final ceremonial football game. (For a description of this ritual, see Jackson 2000.) This game takes place annually on the afternoon prior to the first all-night Stomp Dance of the year. It is customary to hold a pot-luck dinner between the game and the dance; members and the ground's guests from other communities are involved in the dinner. The chief's speaker usually makes a talk or offers a prayer before the meal begins. Sometimes a different man, perhaps one being groomed to become a speaker, will be asked to offer these remarks. On the Saturday in question, the ground's chief, Simon Harry, spoke briefly for himself.[2]

Chief Harry called for the group's attention. He then stated, "In all of my years as a member of this ground, a woman has never been asked to give the blessing over the meal. So today, I have asked my daughter to do this for us." He then gave the nod to one of his three middle-aged daughters, all of whom are active in the ceremonial ground's life. She then delivered a beautiful prayer in the style common to Yuchi ceremonialists, a style that appears to be linked to prayer styles typical of both the Native American Church in Oklahoma and to the practice of Yuchi Methodism. In light of an interest in gendered practices among the Yuchi, Chief Harry's metacommentary suggests slow changes in women's roles in the conservative sector of Yuchi community life. What fixed this incident in my memory was the fact that it was quite remarkably repeated soon after at the Polecat Ceremonial Ground. As a fieldworker interested in the whole of the Yuchi community, I was the only person living in Yuchi country during those years who regularly attended these afternoon meals at both the Duck Creek and Polecat ceremonial grounds, so I was the only person present on both occasions. In this second instance, the Chief of the Polecat ground called upon its eldest member, Mrs. Viola Thomas, to give the blessing. I thought it strange that such a novel moment would happen independently in the same context in two communities in the same season. This case of prayer suggests to me the cautious but discernible form change is taking in the gender relationships between Yuchi ceremonial ground men and women.

Outside the bounds of specifically Yuchi community life, Yuchi men and women participate in the broader American social world. They are conservative in the conscious choices they make to allow this larger world to impact the institutions that help define them as a people, but they are far from isolated from their non-Yuchi neighbors. Earlier studies of Yuchi social life, particularly those by Ballard and Buckley, have made important contributions to an anthropological literature aimed at understanding the complexities inherent in the structural continuities in Yuchi life and changes wrought by internal and external social forces. My contention here and elsewhere (Jackson and Linn 2000) is that a discourse-centered approach to culture, as a tool for a more general program of collaborative ethnography with the Yuchi people, can enrich both the anthropology of the Native people of the Southeast and the broader cross-cultural study of gender and its place in social life.

NOTES

My studies among the Yuchi (1993–present) have been fostered and encouraged by members of the Yuchi tribe, particularly the leaders and members of the three ceremonial ground communities. Newman Littlebear has been among my foremost teachers in matters of Yuchi custom, and I treasure his friendship. That the Yuchi have allowed my family to participate personally in their community life has been a priceless gift and an immense courtesy. Practical support for my studies has also come from the Wenner-Gren Foundation for Anthropological Research, the American Philosophical Society, the Jacobs Fund of the Whatcom Museum, the Central States Anthropological Society, Indiana University, and Gilcrease Museum.

1. Some basic material presented by Buckley stands in more immediate need of correction. Yuchi patrilineal chief and warrior societies, in which men are divided in a dual division pattern, have not disappeared as Buckley suggests (1989:291). They remain important today, determining eligibility to fulfill various political and ritual offices (Jackson 1996).

Buckley (1989:291, 295) apparently accepts Ballard's (1978) statement that a woman was (s)elected as tribal chief in 1956; the Yuchi themselves dispute this claim. The Yuchi are not known to have had at any point in their recent history an overarching tribal chieftainship; they functioned with only local town chiefs, who have always been men. Statements and representations to the contrary are grounded in unsupported (and untruthful) claims by a handful of Yuchi individuals in their dealings with non-Yuchis. The claims of the family associated with the supposed woman chief of 1956 are uniformly discredited by recognized Yuchi political and ritual leaders, including the three town chiefs. The claims themselves form the punchline to a Yuchi running joke about the so-called Yuchi "queens" of such interest to non-Yuchis.

Prior to and after the Ribbon Dance, the women dancers at all Yuchi ceremonial grounds are seated on benches *adjacent* to the south "warrior" arbor, but they do not sit within it as Buckley (1989:307) reports. The women who will participate in the Ribbon Dance eat a meal at the beginning of the Green Corn Ceremonial in the camp of the head woman dancer, which may also be (but is typically not) the camp of the town chief.

Several more complex issues explored by Buckley remain to be reassessed and discussed, but doing so will require more space than the present opportunity provides. An important feature of each of the ethnographic cases discussed in this note is that a picture of pure gender complementarity is undermined and a model of hierarchical reciprocity becomes clearer.

2. Since I was unable to record this brief speech, I must rely on my notes.

REFERENCES

Ballard, W. L. 1978. *The Yuchi Green Corn Ceremonial: Form and Meaning.* Los Angeles: American Indian Studies Center, University of California at Los Angeles.

Bauman, R., and C. L. Briggs. 1990. Poetics and Performance as Critical Perspectives on Language and Social Life. *Annual Review of Anthropology* 19:59–88.

Bell, A. R. 1990. Separate People: Speaking of Creek Men and Women. *American Anthropologist* 92:332–45.

Boas, F. 1940. Introduction to [the] *International Journal of American Linguistics.* In *Race, Language, and Culture,* ed. F. Boas. 199–210. New York: Free Press.

Buckley, T. 1989. The Articulation of Gender Symmetry in Yuchi Culture. *Semiotica* 74:289–311.

Chafe, W. L. 1993. Seneca Speaking Styles and the Location of Authority. In *Responsibility and Evidence in Oral Discourse,* ed. J. H. Hill and J. T. Irvine, pp. 72–87. New York: Cambridge University Press.

Darnell, R. 1999. Theorizing Americanist Anthropology: Continuities from the

B. A. E. to the Boasians. In *Theorizing Americanist Anthropology*, ed. L. P. Valentine and R. Darnell. 38–51. Toronto: University of Toronto Press.

DuBois, J. W. 1986. Self-Evidence and Ritual Speech. In *Evidentiality: The Linguistic Coding of Epistemology*, ed. W. L. Chafe and J. Nichols. 313–36. Norwood, N.J.: Ablex.

Fogelson, R. D. 1977. Cherokee Notions of Power. In *The Anthropology of Power*, ed. R. D. Fogelson and R. N. Adams. 185–94. New York: Academic Press.

———. 1990. On the "Petticoat Government" of the Eighteenth-Century Cherokee. In *Personality and the Cultural Construction of Society: Papers in Honor of Melford E. Spiro*, ed. D. K. Jordan and M. J. Swartz. 161–81. Tuscaloosa: University of Alabama Press.

Goffman, E. 1981. *Forms of Talk*. Philadelphia: University of Pennsylvania Press.

Howard, J. H. 1981. *Shawnee: The Ceremonialism of a Native Indian Tribe and Its Cultural Background*. Athens: Ohio University Press.

Jackson, J. B. 1996. "Everybody Has a Part, Even the Little Bitty Ones": Notes on the Social Organization of Yuchi Ceremonialism. *Florida Anthropologist* 49:121–30.

———. 1998a. The Work of Tradition in Yuchi Oratory. *Florida Anthropologist* 50:197–202.

———. 1998b. Yuchi Ritual. Ph.D. dissertation, Indiana University.

———. 2000. Signaling the Creator: Indian Football as Ritual Performance among the Yuchi and Their Neighbors. *Southern Folklore* 57:33–64.

Jackson, J. B., and M. S. Linn. 2000. Calling in the Members: Linguistic Form and Cultural Context in a Yuchi Ritual Speech Genre. *Anthropological Linguistics* 42:61–80.

Jakobson, R. 1990. The Concept of Mark. In *On Language*, ed. R. Jakobson. 134–40. Cambridge, Mass.: Harvard University Press.

Lévi-Strauss, C. 1944a. On Dual Organization in South America. *América Indígena* 4:37–47.

———. 1944b. Reciprocity and Hierarchy. *American Anthropologist* 46:266–68.

———. 1963. Do Dual Organizations Exist? In *Structural Anthropology*, ed. C. Lévi-Strauss, trans. C. Jacobson and B. G. Schoepf. 132–63. New York: Basic Books.

Reichard, G. A. 1944. *Prayer: The Compulsive Word*. Seattle: University of Washington Press.

Sherzer, J. 1987. A Discourse-Centered Approach to Language and Culture. *American Anthropologist* 89:295–309.

Speck, F. G. 1909. *Ethnology of the Yuchi Indians*. Philadelphia: University Museum, University of Pennsylvania.

Swanton, J. R. 1928. *Religious Beliefs and Medical Practices of the Creek Indians*. Washington, D.C.: Bureau of American Ethnology.

Urban, G. 1991. *A Discourse-Centered Approach to Culture*. Austin: University of Texas Press.

Voegelin, C. F. 1936. *The Shawnee Female Deity*. New Haven, Conn.: Yale University Press.

Yanagisako, S., and J. Collier. 1994. Gender and Kinship Reconsidered: Toward a Unified Analysis. In *Assessing Cultural Anthropology*, ed. R. Borofsky. 190–200. New York: McGraw-Hill.

The Twentieth-Century Conservators
of the Cherokee Sacred Formulas

Willard Walker

James Mooney acquired Cherokee sacred formulas in 1887 and 1888 at
Big Cove in North Carolina, the first white person to do so. He subse-
quently published them (Mooney 1891; Mooney and Olbrechts 1932).
Other formulas have since been published in English translation, if not
in syllabics or transcription. Mooney (1891:307–9) notes that the original manuscripts "were written by the shamans of the tribe, for their own
use, in the Cherokee characters invented by Sikwa'ya [Sequoyah] in
1821, and were obtained, with the explanations, either from the writers
themselves or from their surviving relatives."

The shamans were at first understandably reluctant to give Mooney
their formulas. Mooney asked one of them, Swimmer by name, to sing
a bear-hunting song one day, but Swimmer "made some excuse and was
silent" (1891:311). Mooney and his interpreter met again with Swimmer
the next day when no other Cherokee were present. According to
Mooney (1891:311),

> Swimmer was told that if he persisted in his refusal it would be nec-
> essary to employ someone else, as it was unfair [of] him to furnish
> incomplete information when he was paid to tell all he knew. He
> replied that he was willing to tell anything in regard to stories and
> customs, but that the bear songs were part of his secret knowledge
> and commanded a high price from the hunters. . . . He was told that
> the only object in asking about the songs was to put them on record
> and preserve them, so that when he and the half dozen old men of
> the tribe were dead the world might be aware how much the Chero-
> kees had known. This appeal to his professional pride proved effec-
> tual, and when he was told that a great many similar songs had been

sent to Washington by medicine men of other tribes, he promptly declared that he knew as much as any of them, and that he would give all the information in his possession.

When Swimmer's competitors heard that he had given formulas to Mooney, they impugned his professional integrity, which prompted him to turn over his whole book of formulas and to tell Mooney proudly, "Look at that and now see if I don't know something" (1891:311).

When Mooney had examined his book, Swimmer agreed to sell it to him, but only after he had copied the formulas for his own use. The book became the basis for the transcriptions, translations, and explanations of the ninety-six formulas in *The Swimmer Manuscript* (Mooney and Olbrechts 1932). Mooney then tried to buy the papers of a deceased shaman named Gatigwanasti from his son, who at first declined to sell because he wanted to learn to use them himself and because "they might fall into the hands of Swimmer, who, he was determined, should never see his father's papers" (Mooney 1891:312–13). Mooney (1891:313) claimed that when he returned to Big Cove in 1888, the Cherokee had concluded that "instead of taking this knowledge away from them and locking it up in a box, the intention was to preserve it to the world and pay them for it at the same time. In addition the writer took every opportunity to impress on them the fact that he was acquainted with the secret knowledge of other tribes and perhaps could give them as much as they gave." Gatigwanasti's son ultimately "consented to lend the papers for a time, and after repeated efforts during a period of several weeks, the matter ended in the purchase of the papers outright, with unreserved permission to show them for copying or explanation to anybody who might be selected" (Mooney 1891:313). In the end, all the living shamans and the surviving heirs of those recently deceased turned their formulas over to Mooney, evidently expecting to have their expertise acknowledged if they did so and fearing to be maligned and discredited if they did not.

Robert Conley, writing in 1995, dismissed Mooney as a nineteenth-century ethnologist who "approached his subject with the paternalistic skepticism typical of his contemporary colleagues" (Kilpatrick and Kilpatrick 1995:xi). Mooney's methods, by modern standards at least, were scarcely ethical. But no one to this day has attained the level of rapport that Mooney enjoyed with the Cherokee shamans. Frans Olbrechts (Mooney and Olbrechts 1932:vii) said that when he went to Qualla in

1926 to continue Mooney's work, he found that "the mere statement that I came to stay with them with the same purpose in view as had [Mooney] served as the best introduction I could have desired. People who looked askance, and medicine men who looked sullen when first approached, changed as if touched by a magic wand as they heard his name and as I explained my connection with his work." Leonard Broom (Speck and Broom 1983:xviii), who was at Qualla in 1935 and 1936, wrote that Mooney hired Will West Long "as scribe, aide, and interpreter, but he was far more than an employer. He was West Long's mentor and friend. West Long learned the complex skills of communication across languages, and he was socialized in scholarly attitudes towards his own culture and an inquiring appreciation of it. . . . Thus his association with Mooney set a style of interaction that benefited later scholars for whom West Long served as informant, not in the narrow sense but as a guide and scholarly collaborator." Jack and Anna Kilpatrick (1965:40), who were in Qualla in the 1950s, wrote that "no ethnologist was ever accepted by the Cherokees as was James Mooney. . . . We remember asking an aged member of the Eastern Band, some thirty years after Mooney's death . . . if he had ever heard of the scientist. The sound of that name put fire in his old eyes. 'Hear of him? I knew him!' he stated, with a lift of the chin."

The formulas obtained by Mooney in the 1880s have been recycled by various twentieth-century writers. Frans Olbrechts completed Mooney's work on 96 of the 137 formulas obtained from Swimmer, publishing them in *The Swimmer Manuscript*. Although Mooney had published several love magic formulas in *Sacred Formulas of the Cherokees* (1891:375–84), he intended to publish next "only the formulas that were of a strictly medicinal character, [withholding] all other formulas . . . for publication at some future time" (Mooney and Olbrechts 1932:2). Some Cherokee sacred formulas are clearly therapeutic, some clearly destructive, even homicidal, and many are inherently both therapeutic and destructive, since they are designed to relieve a patient by transferring the malady to his attacker. In conformity with Mooney's intention, the ninety-six formulas published by Olbrechts are all therapeutic in nature.

One of Mooney's formulas was used for men who were about to go to war, appearing in transcriptions, translation, and with extensive notes in *The Sacred Formulas* (1891:388–91). Mooney's English translation of this formula was reproduced (inaccurately and incompletely) by Stan Steiner (1968:1–2), who, in a footnote, credits Mooney as the source and tells us that "Cherokees believe it is sacrilegious for a non-Cherokee to publish, print, or use these sacred formulas. In deference to these fine, deeply religious people I therefore wish to explain that I have merely reprinted them from James Mooney, as he reprinted them from the writing of the Cherokees of the nineteenth century." But Steiner reprinted a fragment of only the English translation, the part in an alien language that the shamans could never have written or read but that was accessible to strangers. In any event, sacrilege cannot be excused on the ground that it merely replicates someone else's prior sacrilege.

In 1969 Rothenberg published his own reformulation of Mooney's (1891:391) translation of what may be the most homicidal of Swimmer's formulas. Mooney's translation consists of one paragraph, 167 words in length, with the title, "To Destroy Life." Rothenberg's (1969:70) version consists of 104 words arranged in seventeen lines under the title, "The Killer." The same reformulation was reprinted in a later work by Rothenberg (1972:62), where it is described as "after A'yunini [Swimmer]" and "Jerome Rothenberg's working, after James Mooney." A note on page 413 acknowledges the same source. Although he was careful to acknowledge both Swimmer and Mooney as his sources, Rothenberg had no compunction about converting into "modern" verse Mooney's translation of a syllabic text written by a man whom he (Rothenberg) had already designated as a "technician of the sacred."

The Kilpatricks published a number of English translations of manuscripts collected by Mooney, but no formulas are among them. Several formulas and many secular documents collected by Mooney in the 1880s have been reproduced in translation and some in transcription by Olbrechts, Speck and Broom, Steiner, Rothenberg, and the Kilpatricks, but only Rothenberg failed to honor Mooney's policy of withholding conjuring formulas from publication. The Kilpatricks, however, violated this restriction in their many publications of sacred formulas obtained in Oklahoma, and in *Friends of Thunder* (1995:193), they published their translation of a therapeutic "conjuration for healing a burn," a footnote to which says that "since we were already familiar with the conjuration, we have taken the liberty of inserting two lines omitted (perhaps intentionally) by the informant."

As noted above, Broom said that Mooney was Will West Long's "mentor and friend," providing him with skills, insights, and attitudes that made him not only a knowledgeable informant but a resourceful colleague with a formidable native intellect. Olbrechts (Mooney and Olbrechts 1932:9) said of three informants, including West Long, that "one is at a loss what to praise most in them—their immense fund of knowledge or the keenness and the interest they manifested in the work." Both Witthoft (1948) and Broom (Speck and Broom 1983:xx) have pointed out, however, that Olbrechts made demeaning, even libelous statements about West Long in *The Swimmer Manuscript*, which were read by West Long and all his relatives soon after the publication of that volume. According to Olbrechts (Mooney and Olbrechts 1934:110), "[Will West Long] is very conceited. He is feared by many, despised by a few, loved by none. . . . I am sure that many times he has by occult means tried to remove from his path and from this world, those that were his avowed or secret enemies. . . . As to his professional honesty, I found several proofs of this being scant indeed. . . . His pronounced erotic nature . . . is undoubtedly responsible for many traits in his behavior; his natural disposition for conceit, e.g., is considerably enhanced by it." Olbrechts made a great show of disguising West Long's true identity and did not refer to him by name in this passage, but only by the initial "W." Nevertheless, the photograph of West Long on plate 5, opposite page 9, is captioned, "W. Main Informant and Interpreter," leaving little doubt as to the identity of the conceited, erotic, feared, unloved, and professionally dishonest conjuror referred to as "W."

The Kilpatricks (1965:viii) have assured us that little remains of a once extensive Cherokee manuscript literature. They say that the few documents that survived are housed in the Bureau of American Ethnology, the library of the American Philosophical Society, the library of the University of Oklahoma, the Thomas Gilcrease Museum, and their own private collection. The latter contained five manuscript versions of a formula called "the Cherokee National Ritual" (Kilpatrick and Kilpatrick 1964) that had been the property of Anna Kilpatrick's great-uncle, an Oklahoma shaman. *The Shadow of Sequoyah* (1965:70) contains translations of two love incantations said to be in the collection of the authors. Both are conjuring formulas that Mooney would have withheld from publication. Another fifty of their formulas appear in their *Notebook of a Cherokee Shaman* (1970). They were obtained in 1961 from the widow of their author (Kilpatrick and Kilpatrick 1970:84) and are given in transcription and translation followed by commentary. Several are conjuring formulas of the sort that Mooney declined to publish. The one that begins on page 100, for example, is used to produce "a state of ecstatic yearning, an otherworldly melancholia peculiarly Cherokeean [and] is generally attributed to the sorcery of an enemy." The Kilpatricks (1970:85) published both vindictive and therapeutic formulas, assuring their readers that "the texts under consideration here are, from the Cherokee viewpoint, 'dead,' of no effect. Their power passed with their owner." A footnote indicates that dead formulas may be rejuvenated, however, "by a previously unreported ritual whereby the materials, polluted by the death of the one who possessed them, are taken to running water and ceremonially cleansed" (1970:85).

We learn from Alan Kilpatrick that his parents acquired formulas in Oklahoma in the 1960s through one or more native purchasing agents, just as Mooney had gotten them in the 1880s through Will West Long. Jack Kilpatrick's primary informant and agent was known by his English name, Willie Jumper. He was an expert at decoding arcane and cryptic doctor books. The importance of this man's contributions to the Kilpatricks' scholarship is acknowledged in many of their publications, and there can be no doubt that Jumper was as useful to them in recording and interpreting sacred formulas as West Long had been to Mooney and later to Olbrechts. But both men were paid to procure texts from others, and both suffered the consequences. Alan Kilpatrick (1997:134) writes that between 1961 and 1966 a "vigorous correspondence" developed between his late father and his "principal informant," Willie Jumper. The latter, however, made himself unpopular with his own relatives as a result of his book-collecting habit. It seems that Jumper wanted to acquire some "ritual paraphernalia" that had belonged to his deceased father and that was then in the possession of his grandfather. In his letter dated March 6, 1962, he wrote to J. Kilpatrick that his grandfather not only declined to part with these items but said, "Well he said not to come Back anymore his place" (A. Kilpatrick 1997:135).

In 1963 Willie Jumper tried to buy formulas from an elder whom he described as a "cranky old man" but to whom he reluctantly paid an exorbitant price for his notebooks because "I begin thought he might cong me." On his way home a spindle bolt broke and his car went off the road. He wrote on July 17, "I think Something wrong with me. I do Believe Someone must Be doing Some conging me" (A. Kilpatrick 1997:135).

Will West Long and Willie Jumper both decided, independently of one another, to seek out formulas and make them available to scholars despite the overt and covert hostility of their respective relatives, neighbors, and professional competitors. They chose to save what they could for future generations. But Olbrechts betrayed his loyal scribe, interpreter, and purchasing agent; Steiner broke up a formula, took the pieces out of context, and published an inaccurate English translation; Rothenberg did likewise; the Kilpatricks restored the lines omitted from a text; Jack Kilpatrick sent Willie Jumper after sacred things in the safekeeping of his father's father, who told him not to come back. Alan Kilpatrick published a book that compromises the reputations of both his parents and their agent.

I close with a passage from the introduction to Speck and Broom's *Cherokee Dance and Drama* (1983:1), a work originally written in 1951 with the collaboration of Will West Long: "Like all outsiders coming to the Cherokee, in truth like the prototypes of the Boogers themselves, we often appear in their midst uninvited, seeking something to exploit. Like the Boogers, with unmannerly insistence we ethnologists break into Cherokee home circles at the height of their social festivities. Politely these people tolerate our intrusion until, our desires gratified, we depart."

REFERENCES

Kilpatrick, Alan. 1997. *The Night Has a Naked Soul: Witchcraft and Sorcery among the Western Cherokee.* Syracuse, N.Y.: Syracuse University Press.
Kilpatrick, Jack F., and Anna G. Kilpatrick. 1964. "The Foundation of Life": The Cherokee National Ritual. *American Anthropologist* 66(1):1386–91.
———. 1965. *The Shadow of Sequoyah: Social Documents of the Cherokees, 1862–1964.* Norman: University of Oklahoma Press.
———. 1970. *Notebook of a Cherokee Shaman.* Washington, D.C.: Smithsonian Institution Press.
———. 1995. *Friends of Thunder: Folktales of the Oklahoma Cherokees.* Norman: University of Oklahoma Press.
Mooney, James. 1891. *The Sacred Formulas of the Cherokees.* Washington, D.C.: Smithsonian Institution, Bureau of American Ethnology.
Mooney, James, and Frans Olbrechts. 1932. *The Swimmer Manuscript: Cherokee Sacred Formulas and Medicinal Prescriptions.* Washington, D.C.: Smithsonian Institution, Bureau of American Ethnology.

Rothenberg, Jerome. 1969. *Technicians of the Sacred: A Range of Poetries from Africa, America, Asia, and Oceania.* Garden City, N.Y.: Doubleday.

———. 1972. *Shaking the Pumpkin: Traditional Poetry of the North American Indians.* Garden City, N.Y.: Doubleday.

Speck, Frank G., and Leonard Broom. 1983 [1951]. *Cherokee Dance and Drama.* Berkeley: University of California Press.

Steiner, Stan. 1968. *The New Indians.* New York: Harper and Row.

Witthoft, John. 1948. Will West Long, Cherokee Informant. *American Anthropologist* 50:355–59.

Stress and Coping among Chickasaw Indian Fathers: Lessons for Indian Adolescents and Their Counselors in Treatment for Substance Abuse

Lisa J. Lefler

The American Indian Fatherhood Project[1] was a two-year study funded by a grant from the Maternal and Child Health Bureau. The University of Oklahoma's Health Promotion Programs[2] partnered with four Oklahoma tribal communities—the Kiowa, Ft. Sill Apache, Comanche, and Chickasaw Nations—to begin this first in-depth ethnographic study of Indian fatherhood. One hundred and seventy-one Indian men and women were interviewed on the second of two formal interview sessions of the study. At the time of this writing, only data from twenty-nine of the fifty Chickasaw men had been analyzed. This essay therefore focuses only on this small sample of tribally enrolled fathers, aged twenty-four to seventy-nine, who were interviewed regarding their perceptions of stress and coping strategies. For the purposes of this essay, the analysis will divide the sample into two groups: younger [y] (n=15) and older [o] (n=13).[3] The cut-off point was determined by the age of the youngest veteran to have served in a war zone, which was forty-four.

Each participant in the study was interviewed at least twice within a year and a half, with two different interview instruments. The second instrument, which is the one I will emphasize in this analysis, addresses the issues of bicultural identity and stress. Questions concerning stress derived from former experience working with Indian adolescents in treatment for substance abuse, field experience with Indian families, and input and discussions with Indian men and counselors who have dealt with issues of post-traumatic stress disorder (PTSD). Clinically oriented questions were modified from the diagnostic criteria for PTSD, numbered 309.81 in the *DSM-IV Guidebook* (Frances, First, and Pincus 1995).

One of the objectives of focusing on stress in this study was to see if there are adult coping mechanisms or factors that might be modified and shared with Indian youth who have been identified as "at risk" for maladaptive behavior(s). My experience with Indian youth in treatment for substance abuse has indicated that such information could prove beneficial in dealing with kids' exposure to violence and stressful family and community situations. A family therapist from a regional Indian youth treatment center with whom I spoke expressed the hope that our research could shed some light on how to address the stress and trauma that impacts Indian adolescents. She told me: "These kids haven't been through war, but the experiences these kids are having are traumatic, yet they are normalized by the community and the profession. People can't see the forest for trees, you know. This goes hand in hand with abuse and violence—people don't raise their eyebrows about it any more. People are more desensitized to the trauma of it and don't even see it or feel it." Preliminary results from the fatherhood study indicated that a significant percentage of Chickasaw men in this group have also experienced trauma or times of extraordinary stress. When asked if they had ever been physically attacked, 45 percent of the men responded in the affirmative. Just over 86 percent said they had been in a situation where their own or someone else's life had been in danger. Only four of the men had ever served in a war zone, and yet almost 59 percent of them said they had been threatened with a weapon. When asked if they had ever experienced a traumatic event, there was no significant difference between the older men (including war veterans) and the younger men (y=84.6%, o=86.7%), while 79.3% of all the men stated that they had seen at least one person seriously injured or killed. About 34 percent of the men said they had been separated from their families for an extended period in the past; 38 percent had experienced a life-threatening illness (mostly as children), while 31 percent had experienced a fire, flood, or other natural disaster (mostly tornadoes, living as they do in the part of the country often referred to as "Tornado Alley"). Older men, however, were significantly more likely to have experienced natural disasters than younger men (46.2% vs. 13.3%).

As data analysis began, it was clear that there were some significant differences between the younger and older men in terms of how they perceived and quantified stress. The data seemed to suggest that older Chickasaw men have developed better skills to cope with stress than have the younger men in the sample. For example, statistically significant responses included those younger men who said that they were nervous most of the time (y=33.3% vs. o=7.7%, s=.053); said they had repeated disturbing memories (y=20% vs. o=7.7%, s=.088); had repeated disturbing dreams (y=20% vs. o=0%, s=.040); were more likely to be extremely upset when reminded of a stressful event (y=33.3% vs. o=7.7%, s=.072); experienced a greater loss of interest in activities that they used to enjoy (y=26.7% vs. o=7.7%, s=.025); and were much more likely to have irritable or angry outbursts (y=26.6% vs. o=0%, s=.005).

Comparing younger men to older men who were not veterans actually created greater statistical differences in some categories. Younger men indicated that they had a harder time falling asleep (y=26.7% vs. o=0%, s=.094); were less comfortable around people (y=26.7% vs. o=0%, s=.004); responded affirmatively when asked if they had been physically attacked or abused (y=60% vs. o=0%, s=.000); were more likely to have been physically abusive in the past (y=26.7% vs. o=0%, s=.004); were more likely to have been separated from their families for an extended period of time in the past (y=46.7% vs. o=0%, s=.050); and said that they would rather be by themselves (y=33.3% vs. o=11.1%, s=.004).

Younger men were less likely to have felt calm (y=13.3% vs. o=0%, s=.004); more likely to experience nervousness (y=33.3% vs. o=11.1%, s=.087); more likely to have felt so down in the dumps that nothing could cheer them up (y=13.4% vs. o=0%, s=.018); more likely to be upset or reminded of a stressful event (y=26.6% vs. o=0%, s=.000); more likely to experience a physical reaction when reminded of a stressful experience (y=33.3% vs. o=0%, s=.040); more likely to avoid activities or situations because they were reminded of stressful experience(s) (y=6.7% vs. 0=0%, s=.072); more likely to express a loss of interest in activities they used to enjoy (y=26.7% vs. o=0%, s=.006); more likely to express feeling emotionally numb (y=6.7% vs. o=0%, s=.009); more likely to have irritable or angry outbursts (y=26.6% vs. o=0%, s=.001); and more likely to say that they had difficulty concentrating (y=13.3% vs. o=0%, s=.052). Moreover, the younger men felt that the future would somehow be cut short (y=33.3% vs. o=0%, s=.009). They also had a more difficult time being intimate with their partners (y=33.4% vs. o=0%, s=.013) and their children (y=13.4% vs. o=0%, s=.058).

I want to emphasize that these are descriptive, not parametric statistics; therefore, it cannot be said that these are responses generalizable to all Chickasaw men. I have no reason, however, to think that these patterns are not representative of the community. More to the point, the differences between the two subgroups in this sample are not due to chance. These findings are only first steps in the analysis of the massive quantity of data received from these communities. We must also review responses for an additional twenty-one Chickasaw men and twenty-one Chickasaw women, plus one hundred Kiowa, Ft. Sill Apache, and Comanche men and women.

To get a better sense of the context from which these answers came, the second portion of this essay focuses on the transcribed narratives of the interviews. When answering if they felt they had more or less stress than most people, most of the men said they felt they had less. Most of them responded in a stoic way, saying they realized that they "had to learn to deal with life without stressing out about it." They seemed to have the idea that things happen the way they are supposed to, and one just has to realize that one cannot change the course of events.

When asked what things in life were most stressful, the majority of men said they were concerned for their children. Some were also stressed because they did not have access to their children. Several of the men stated that they were separated or divorced and did not have their children with them. At a later time, when we have analyzed all of the first-round data concerning family union and dissolution, we will be better able to correlate the exact percentage of men who are divorced and separated and calculate how many men are not living with some or all of their children.

Even though there are many stories about witnessing horrible car accidents, fights in bars, seeing people die, and racial discrimination, the narratives seem to indicate that the men perceive their greatest source of stress and trauma as stemming from family separation or regrets about not having been a better father. Some of the men were worried about how their children were doing because they were separated from the children's mothers, who had custody; some of the children also resided with grandparents. Others had children or grandchildren who were deceased. Over half of the men stated that they had been threatened with a weapon, and 86 percent of them had seen death or traumatic events; yet it was familial relationships that had impacted them the most. The most stressful issues were those concerning the welfare of their children.

One man, forty-one years old, explained why he could not get emotionally close to his wife or sons at all: "Oh I can get close to them and then, I don't. I try not to because I know that my sons and my wife, if I get in her business, ya know, then I try to find out what's going on, ya know, she kinda gets upset. Starts into an argument, so I try not to push, uh push it too much. If I push, she'll get upset, start a real argument and I don't wanna argue with her. Nobody don't understand how I feel . . . 'cause I don't tell 'em my problems." Another of the interviewees stated that he "keeps his distance from others." Later in the interview, he acknowledged that he felt that people had let him down, and he felt that he couldn't trust people. This individual's secondary occupation was as a minister. He also provided several recent examples of his experience with racism and discrimination. Not only did he talk about how white people stereotyped all Indians; he also complained about how some Indian people discriminated against other Indians: "You know I've always wanted someone to explain to me, well, what it is to be an Indian. You know exactly what isn't it . . . ya know, ya hear 'that's not, that ain't Indian, . . . somebody's ways may not be, ya know.' Well, what is an Indian? It makes you wonder if they even know theirself. Ya know, like I said, there's just levels of it. Fullblood'll look down on me 'cause I'm mixed blood, fullblood'll look down on another fullblood 'cause he don't speak his language." Regardless of what was said during the initial interviews, a majority of the men still claimed that they felt they had less stress in their life than most other people. A frequent qualifier for this statement was, "It's just how you handle it." For example, a man, thirty-four years old, reflected on his younger days:

When I was younger, I used to think I had a lot of stress, 'cause my dad was an alcoholic, or rather he would drink a lot, and my mom was always off working trying to support us kids. So I was left up to me. My dad was a truck driver and was gone most of the time. I really didn't think about it because I didn't know any better . . . and I was taking care of my younger brother and sister. And having to go to school and sometimes we'd come back, we didn't have nothing to eat, 'cause my mom having to come back on weekends and Dad would be gone sometimes a couple of weeks. . . . So whenever I started thinking about it, I used to have a lot on my shoulders, then I started realizing that there's a lot more people out there that had it a lot worse than I did, so I grew outta that. I guess I've got a lot of stress, but it's not nothing that I shouldn't be able to handle, it's just how you deal with it. I read a lot of books and watch movies and come home and watch TV, just to get my mind off of things.

Another man, fifty-four years old, responded that it was the support network that he had built up that helped him reduce his stress. He also spoke indirectly about regularly attending church. This individual had a clinical illness that had caused a previous marriage to fail, and numerous tragedies had compounded that illness. Nevertheless, he now feels that he has turned things around as he is remarried and trying to raise two sets of kids.

Others recount traumatic events in great detail, although they do not reveal their strategies for coping. For example, one man, fifty-nine years old, described seeing a friend shoot and kill his wife. "Uh, I guess I didn't really, you know, I was young at the time and it bothered me somewhat for a day or so, but it went away." When asked if that had been the only time he had seen someone killed, he described a second incident: "I think it was Thanksgiving, some of the kin came over and they was all at the kitchen table. The mother got up and she said she wasn't feeling good, she wanted to lay down. So after that her husband went in there and the next thing ya heard was a shotgun shot. And the only part I could see was, ya know, they had the curtains drawn and, ya know, how kids get up to the window and look through the cracks, you could see where it blew her head off right across through the neck. . . . That's about the worst thing I've seen." When asked about dealing with stressful experiences, he continued, "If something comes up, ya know, to make me feel bad or something, I usually try to think it out as soon as I can and then get rid of that feeling and go on to something else. I mean I don't usually let anything bother me if I can help it."

Most of these men spoke of handling stress or learning to deal with it, and many referred to the inevitability of trauma—that's just the way it is, and "getting stressed ain't gonna help none," as a forty-one-year-old man put it. He continued by saying, "Might as well just deal with it and go on. Maybe later in life it'll work its way out, that's the way I see it." From those older Chickasaw men who have experienced trauma and seemed to have, in their own words, "dealt with it," there seems to emanate a vital sense of adaptability and resiliency. One man, seventy-two years of age, said, "I just live, like the Good Book [said], livin' day to day and when things happen to you, it's what the Good Lord intended, it's the way it was gonna happen. Ain't no way . . . as like when a man's time comes, that's it, that's it, no way to save yourself."

I spoke with a Kiowa who is a counselor and is well known in the area for his experience and expertise concerning PTSD among Indian men. He has found in his years of counseling that ceremony and ritual are the most significant intervention strategies. He finds that Indian men who are dealing with PTSD and who participate in the peyote rituals of the Native American Church, sweat lodge, and/or Sun Dance ceremonies, use these activities as coping mechanisms. In a similar fashion, we find that many Chickasaws use church attendance as a support mechanism. The reality of extreme trauma and exposure to violence, however, seems to be compartmentalized among many of the Chickasaw men. Compartmentalizing, or "normalizing" traumatic experiences can be a common practice (Briere 1997; Manson et al. 1996). I therefore inquired about coping strategies in an interview with an Indian health professional who had worked with the Chickasaws as well as with other tribal people. He told me: "Many of these men are self-medicating via alcohol and other substances. The older men had probably 'shut down,' and were not emotionally attached to these disturbing experiences. The younger men are still in the process of desensitizing themselves and probably vocalize their experiences more. But as we [Indian people] understand being part of a circle of life, the denial of their pain and their anger will show itself within the circle. It eventually comes out, and unfortunately among our youth." What can we learn from talking with these Indian men and fathers? What lessons can be transferred to assist addiction counselors with Indian youth? American Indians are not a homogeneous people, and therefore the experiences of Chickasaw men should not be generalized to all Indian men and fathers. We can, however, learn from the voices of these men and hope that their shared experiences can inform others who work with Native youth and fathers. For example:

Take careful note of exposure to violence (e.g., at what age, what type), because such exposure might contribute to young men's need to self-medicate, to become "numbed."

Deal with sources of anger, shame, and guilt as soon as possible.

Try to build a support network during treatment and for aftercare when the young men return to their homes and communities; for example, establish a mentoring program.

Try to connect important lessons for young people with formal ceremony/ritual that makes the learning experiential rather than just words without meaning.

Fathers need to be careful in evaluating the factors that impacted the men who were fathers to them, in considering the generational history of men in their families, and then in examining their own attitudes about fathering (e.g., consider the impact of boarding schools and of violent experiences).

Try to make special efforts to provide positive male modeling. Many of the men in this study felt that their greatest source of stress came from being separated from their children. Developing good parenting workshops with Indian trainers who can share their expertise may provide a way for young fathers to learn about what is involved in fatherhood and also find support from the other men in attendance.

Have successfully recovering men from the community come to treatment to talk to young men about their experiences and journeys to wellness.

John Red Horse (1980) has pointed out that when it comes to American Indians, heritage, custom, and family are interwoven. It is therefore critical when working with fathers and young men to understand the importance and impact of history in contemporary families and to rely on the strengths built into the extended family system to address the needs of young people.

NOTES

1. The American Indian Fatherhood Project is supported by grant MCJ-400827 from the Maternal and Child Health Bureau (Title V, Social Security Act), Health Resources and Services Administration, Department of Health and Human Services.

2. My thanks and deepest appreciation for support and continued guidance for this project go to the Chickasaw Nation of Oklahoma, the Ft. Sill Apache Tribe of Oklahoma, the Kiowa Tribe of Oklahoma, the Comanche Nation of Oklahoma, and Billy Rogers, Health Promotion Programs, University of Oklahoma. I would also like to acknowledge and thank the staff and counselors of the Unity Regional Youth Treatment Center in Cherokee, North Carolina, for their continued insight and guidance concerning these important issues that impact American Indian youth and families.

3. One man's age was not indicated.

REFERENCES

Briere, John. 1997. *Psychological Assessment of Adult Post-traumatic Stress.* Washington, D.C.: American Psychological Association.

Frances, Allen, M. B. First, and H. A. Pincus. 1995. *DSM-IV Guidebook: The Essential Companion to the Diagnostic and Statistical Manual of Mental Disorders.* 4th ed. Washington, D.C.: American Psychological Association.

Manson, S., J. Beals, T. O'Neill, J. Piasecki, D. Bechtold, E. Keane, and M. Jones. 1996. Wounded Spirits, Ailing Hearts: PTSD and Related Disorders among American Indians. In *Ethnocultural Aspects of Post-traumatic Stress Disorder: Issues, Research, and Clinical Applications*, ed. A. J. Marsella, M. J. Friedman, E. T. Gerrity, and R. M. Scurfield. 255–84. Washington, D.C.: American Psychological Association.

Red Horse, John. 1980. American Indian Families: Research Perspectives. In *The American Indian Family: Strengths and Stress*, ed. Fred Hoffman. 1–11. Isleta, N.M.: American Indian Social Research and Development Associates, Inc.

The American Indian Fatherhood Project: The Impact of Incarceration on Chickasaw Fathers

Donald Shannon

Work on the American Indian Fatherhood Project consisted of interviewing Indian men and women concerning their perceptions of fatherhood, roles of fathers, and challenges confronted by American Indian fathers. This essay focuses on the impact of incarceration on Chickasaw[1] men in their roles as fathers, in their relationships with their children, and in their reintegration into society following release. Some preliminary findings and possible implications of these findings will be discussed. The significance of this research lies in its potentially broad applicability for public policy makers concerned with the development of re-entry programs for American Indian men following release from incarceration.

THE PROJECT

This essay reports on a sub-study of the American Indian Fatherhood Project, which was housed in the Department of Health Promotion Programs at the University of Oklahoma and funded by a grant from the Maternal and Child Health Bureau (grant MCJ-400827). Researchers initiated the project by gathering data on American Indian perspectives toward fathering among the Chickasaw, Kiowa, Comanche, and Ft. Sill Apache of Oklahoma. These four groups represent two distinct culture types, sometimes referred to in Oklahoma as "Western Indians" and "Civilized Tribes." The Chickasaw, like the Apache, were traditionally matrilineal and were farmers in the Southeast with a long history of interaction with whites. The patrilineal tribes of the Plains and Southwest traditionally had a long history of both military and cultural resistance to whites. It is interesting to note that the U.S. Army continues to maintain a large military presence in the heart of this area.

This research is significant in that there is virtually no published material regarding either the cultural aspects of fathering among American Indian men or the intracultural diversity within Indian populations. Because laws that apply to children, fathers, custody, and inheritance are primarily based on the white model of nuclear families, many of these policies may not be culturally appropriate within the context of contemporary Indian life.

This essay takes the initial research a step further: once Chickasaw men had been interviewed for the fatherhood research, a smaller subset of that interview population were asked to share their history of incarceration and its impact on intrafamilial relations, with special attention paid to father-child relations. There is published material available on the general effect of incarceration on father-child relations, but virtually none of it deals specifically with American Indians.

The overall goal of this research is to produce results that can assist tribal governments in lobbying for amendments in policy concerning fathers and families. These amendments would be culturally sensitive and applicable within the context of contemporary Indian life. This essay explores the factors that led Chickasaw men to incarceration, their histories of incarceration, and how incarceration affected fathers' relationships with children. These results should be helpful to tribal, local, state, and federal agencies that deal with family policy and the criminal justice system. I also hope to contribute to our understanding of the types of crimes for which Chickasaw men are being incarcerated and thus separated from their children and families for prolonged periods. Such data should help the relevant authorities develop programs that are preventive in nature.

ETHNOGRAPHIC BACKGROUND

The Chickasaw, whose original home was in northern Mississippi and western Tennessee, were removed to Oklahoma in the 1830s along with the other "Five Civilized Tribes" of the Southeast. Enduring their own

"Trail of Tears," the Chickasaw were placed in the western part of the land originally assigned to the Choctaw, an area today occupying roughly 11.5 counties in south-central Oklahoma. This area is now known as the Chickasaw Nation, defined by the area where tribal services are provided. Its current population and landowners are, however, predominantly non-Indian. According to figures provided to me by the Chickasaw Nation, there were, as of 1998, 37,685 Chickasaw in the United States, of which 24,297 reside in Oklahoma. Only about half of them, however, actually reside in the service area.[2]

The Chickasaw have a long history of intermarriage with Europeans, dating to the 1700s when English traders married Chickasaw women. Their mixedblood children quickly became the elite of the tribe, representing it in dealings with the federal government. This situation has continued into the present; rates of intermarriage seem to be increasing. When Chickasaw in the area of Ada, Oklahoma, were asked why they do not marry other Chickasaw, they most commonly answered that marriage would be impossible because somehow one is related to all other Chickasaw. There are fewer than 400 fullblooded Chickasaw represented in the current tribal census; people who are 1/2048th Chickasaw can still claim membership because, according to the tribal constitution, any person who can trace an ancestor to an original enrollee is recognized by the tribe and (if they request it) assigned a Certificate of Degree of Indian Blood (CDIB) card.

The high rate of intermarriage is associated with a loss of specifically Chickasaw cultural traits. The most obvious area of cultural loss is language; there are only approximately 300 remaining speakers of the Chickasaw language, not all of whom are truly fluent. Most of the Chickasaw speakers are over the age of forty. Language loss may also be attributed to the historical policy of government suppression. When Chickasaw children were sent to boarding schools, they were punished for speaking their native language. Moreover, Chickasaw parents have declined to teach the language to their children even if they themselves were fluent; such parents identified their own lack of fluency in English as a problem in their lives, and they wanted to make sure that their children were primarily proficient in English. Speaking Chickasaw has been seen as an impediment to assimilation and to success in education and employment.

In order to combat cultural loss, some members of the tribe have attempted to revive the Stomp Dance. Some elderly Chickasaw had witnessed and participated in the Stomp Dance as children, but they have not been uniformly enthusiastic about sharing their knowledge with younger people. They say, "Those days are gone, there's no point in trying to bring them back." As a result, the revivalists have, in forming the Chickasaw Nation Dance Troupe (which is composed mainly of people on the tribal payroll), resorted to borrowing dances, songs, and rituals from the Seminole and Creek; the resulting performances are therefore largely unrelated to Chickasaw tradition. There have also been attempts to revive the stickball game, but once again the only people who know how to play are too old to participate and are unwilling to pass on their knowledge. Those who are playing the game now are doing so on the basis of rules and rituals borrowed from neighboring tribes. Even the craft of making ball sticks has been learned from the Seminole and Creek.

Some members of the tribe point out that the growth in tribal enrollment is due, at least in part, to the perceived benefits of being recognized as an Indian, including preference in hiring by both the tribal and federal governments, subsidized medical care, and financial assistance for schooling, home loans, and the purchase of basic commodities. Mixed-blood families continue to hold most of the dominant political positions within the tribe, and there seems to be some feeling that those in power expect the support of the rest of the tribe in return for the granting of those perceived benefits. Some Chickasaw therefore feel alienated from the political process of tribal government and express some bitterness toward "card-carrying Indians" or "paper Indians." Some have expressed the belief that the less Indian "blood" a person has, the more likely he or she is to demand the free services offered by the tribe. There is special bitterness directed toward those who are low on Indian "blood" and who never claimed Indian status before there were identifiable benefits associated with that status. Men talk about boys who used to hurl racial taunts at them in school but who are now working for the tribal government.

The bulk of the research for this project took place in Ada, the administrative seat of the Chickasaw Nation, where both tribal headquarters and at least a half-dozen housing projects serving Indians are located. The Carl Albert Indian Health Facility is also located in Ada; it is one of the hubs for providing medical care to persons who can establish Indian ancestry in Oklahoma. While the population of the geographic area of the Chickasaw Nation is mostly non-Indian, Indians still make up roughly 30 percent of the population of the Ada area. Outside of tribal government, however, identifiable Indians are virtually nonexistent in positions of power in the local hierarchies of politics, education, and law enforcement. For example, Indian students make up 16 percent of the student body of Ada High School, but there are no Indians employed as teachers or coaches according to the school principal, whom I interviewed in March 2000. There are no American Indians (Chickasaw or otherwise) working as patrolmen in the Ada police department, a force of thirty-two officers. (For that matter, there are no African American, Hispanic, or Asian American officers.) There is one dispatcher who identifies as Indian (1/8th Chickasaw). An official of the Ada P.D. told me that he believes there are no Indians working for the department because the Chickasaw Nation employs so many Indians in the area. I was told that it has been difficult to hire and retain minority workers for both the police and fire departments; African Americans are reluctant to move to the predominantly white town, and those with more advanced training in law enforcement are usually hired away by the Oklahoma Highway Patrol, which offers greater pay and a better selection of areas in which to work.

Many men who were identifiably Indian told us in the course of the fatherhood study interviews that they believed the police in Ada targeted them, and other identifiable Indians, for traffic stops, identification checks, and/or outstanding warrant checks. Officers usually claim that when such things happen it is because they were on the lookout for someone fitting the same description. City law in Ada states that anyone who is intoxicated in public can be arrested. "Intoxication" is identified by smelling alcohol on the breath, followed by a field sobriety test administered by an officer. No breathalyzer or other objective tests are administered. "Public" is defined as any area accessible to the public, but in practical terms it means any area outside one's private residence. Indians have reported being arrested on their front porches, while in bars, or while riding in cars even if the drivers thereof are not intoxicated. Many identifiable Indians feel that the police look for reasons to pull them over while letting whites off for the same infractions. Other identifiable Indian men say that police will stop them while they are walking to ask them for identification and then hold them in custody while conducting checks for outstanding warrants.

METHODS

Both qualitative and quantitative data for this project were collected through two extensive sets of interviews, along with participant observation of community events. To be selected for an interview, one had to identify as Chickasaw and have either biological or socially recognized children. All interviews were voluntary and each was audiotaped with informed, signed consent; the interviews were usually conducted at the person's residence or at other tribal places. One of the limitations of the study is that the interviewees were largely self-selected, since there was very little publicity for the project in the local media or by the tribal government. Indeed, interviewees were largely recruited via personal introduction from persons who had already been interviewed, resulting in a large number of participants being related to one another.

 For purposes of this particular essay, eight Chickasaw fathers were interviewed concerning their arrest and incarceration histories. They were also asked to discuss their perceptions of incarceration and the effects their experiences had had on their relationships with their families and children. Two of the eight men were drawn from a pool of men who had been interviewed for the fatherhood project. Since the men were in some cases related to each other, self-selected, and identifiable Indians, this group should not be taken as representative of the Chickasaw.

RESULTS

Of the eight men interviewed, seven had been arrested so many times they could not provide a precise number; most of their offenses were alcohol-related, and the majority of the men still abused alcohol. Only one man saw that his incarceration had had a negative impact on his relationship with his children: while he was incarcerated, his wife divorced him and his children now live with another man they identify as their father. Since he does not own a car and can never again obtain a driver's license, he is very limited in his ability to see his children. The rest of the men seemed not to see any such negative effects, although one of them did see that his son was following in his footsteps. In fact, two of the men had six adult sons between them, two of whom were currently in prison, and five of whom had a history of alcohol use and arrest. The eight participants' stories are summarized as follows:

1. This man has three children. He has been arrested approximately thirty times and incarcerated fifteen times since he was eighteen years old. His incarcerations include overnight stays, stretches of 10, 30, 40, and 53 days, and a 90-day stint in a rehab boot camp. His offenses include an unpaid DUI fine, seven DUIs, twenty acts of public drunkenness, other unpaid fines (including contempt of court), driving while under suspension, and stealing beer. He talks about not being able to spend time with his kids and being unable to work to make money to buy things for his kids. On the other hand, he does not think his problems have been decisive in the lives of his kids, since they have so many other people influencing them. His parents usually kept the children while he was incarcerated, as their mom was not around. One of his sons is now in prison for attempted murder, and two others have done jail time.

2. This man has three girls and a boy. He has been arrested four times and has been in jail four times for alcohol-related offenses, once for knocking a tree down while drunk. His wife and kids visited him while he was in jail, but since he was a trustee they were not too concerned. None of his children has ever been incarcerated.

3. This man has three sons and a daughter. He has been arrested and incarcerated more than eight times since he was thirteen years of age; his time of incarceration includes six months in a military stockade, the result of a court martial for being AWOL. One of his arrests was the result of domestic abuse; while he was drunk and on drugs, he got into a fight with one of his sons. He has also been arrested for nonpayment of child support. He claims that being incarcerated taught him how to deal with people. His kids usually visited while he was locked up, although he would have preferred that they not do so. Two of his sons have been incarcerated.

4. This man has three biological and four socially recognized children. He has been arrested and jailed more than thirty times, for sentences ranging from overnight to twenty-eight months. His offenses include trying to outrun a police officer, numerous DUIs, and assaults. He has never seen much of his children, especially since his divorce. Even after release, he can only see his children if another relative is present.

5. This man has one son. He has been arrested approximately thirty times and been in prison four times, once for twenty-five months. His offenses have been mostly DUIs, with some drug charges and charges for public drunkenness and driving with a suspended license. He is one of the men who claims the local police stop Indians and "do anything they want." He admits that he has not been the father he should have been. His son has been arrested and has spent time in jail. He claims that there is not a lot of shame associated with arrest and incarceration, but he knows he caused his family a lot of worry. He started using alcohol when he was twelve years of age and hung out with the "wrong crowd," most of whom were white. His parents were both alcohol abusers.

6. This man has one child. He has been arrested and incarcerated more times than he can count, although most of them were less than sixty-day sentences. His arrests have been mostly for public intoxication, with a few for DUI and driving without a license. He also did time on one occasion for failing to report a crime. Most of his arrests came before he had a child, but he is aware of having alienated his parents, who did not approve of his drinking.

7. This man has one "social child" (his girlfriend's daughter). He has been arrested too many times to count, and, although he has never been in prison, he has been in the drunk tank "many a time." All of his arrests were alcohol-related. He also spent a night in jail on a rape charge, although the case was soon dropped. He knows he was a "mean drunk," and his stepdaughter "hates" him because of the way he abused her mom. The rest of the family has been unconcerned—they more or less expected him to go wrong. His brother is in jail "all the time."

8. This man has four children. He has spent three years in prison, and has been in county and city jails on numerous occasions. He

blames his divorce on his being gone so much. He can no longer see his children since his ex-wife remarried. He lost his family, his house, and his cars due to incarceration.

DISCUSSION

One of the possible reasons the men tended not to identify negative effects of their incarcerations is their reliance on extended family. While they were in prison, children were turned over to grandparents or other relatives for housing, direct care, role models, and support. It could reasonably be argued that the composition of Chickasaw families is highly flexible, with children commonly residing with persons other than their biological parents. When parents lose custody, tribal agencies prefer to place children in the homes of relatives and will go to great lengths to do so.

Moreover, the men accept binge drinking, frequent arrests, and incarcerations as a normal part of life. I would not go so far as to say that arrest and incarceration are treated as rites of passage, but there can be little argument that it is a common feature of Chickasaw life in Oklahoma. Preliminary results from the fatherhood study indicate that 56 percent of the men have had experience with arrest and incarceration.

There are several important implications of this research. First, there is no program offered by the Chickasaw Nation to re-integrate men back into their communities upon release. It is not clear whether this lapse has had a measurable impact on rates of recidivism, but given the very high number of repeat offenses it is certainly an aspect of policy that calls for critical reexamination. I am unaware of any tribal programs aimed at alcohol prevention. There are no treatment-efficacy outcome data for the tribe's adult drug and alcohol rehabilitation program. Many former clients joke that the first place they go upon getting out of the program is the liquor store. In fact, the tribal legislature in 1999 approved the sale of alcohol in tribally owned businesses. Alcohol is obviously related to various health problems, and often associated with the arrests of the men in the study group. The individual histories show that the men are most often arrested for alcohol-related offenses. A continued prevention program would certainly seem to be called for.

Many of the men were no longer able to obtain driver's licenses or auto insurance, which meant that it was very difficult for them to find employment or visit their families. Indeed, this factor was frequently cited as a reason the men were unable to maintain good relations with their children. The men are limited to areas they can reach on foot or by bicycle and are dependent on friends or family for rides to places further removed. Since many of the men leave jail and return to conditions of poverty, it is not surprising that they return to abusing alcohol and get arrested time and again.

The tribal government found this research useful in identifying the factors that lead Chickasaw men to incarceration and in understanding the effects of incarceration on father-child relations. Chickasaw tribal administrators familiar with these study results are currently developing strategies for a grant proposal to create a culturally appropriate re-entry program. The Chickasaw Nation has reacted quickly to our findings and is trying to find a viable solution that would initiate new programs and link existing tribal agencies so that they can better coordinate their efforts to address these important issues. At a time when increasing media attention is focused on the importance of father presence in child development, this research should contribute to our understanding of the causes of father absence.

NOTES

1. The American Indian Fatherhood Project is greatly indebted to the hospitality and generosity of each of the participating tribal nations. I would particularly like to thank the Chickasaw Indian men and women who graciously consented to discuss these important and sensitive issues. I thank Jay Keel, Administrator of Youth and Family Services, and Daryl Walker, former Director of Family Advocacy for the Chickasaw Nation, for their continued interest and support.

2. Figures are now probably higher. There was an effort in 1999 to encourage people to obtain CDIBs in anticipation of an important tribal government election.

Emahakv Vpelofv (Teaching Hammock): Developing a University/Native American Partnership

Susan E. Stans and Louise Gopher

Emahakv Vpelofv ("teaching hammock" in the Creek language)[1] is a partnership developed between the Seminole Tribe's Parent Advisory Committee at Brighton Reservation and Florida Gulf Coast University (FGCU) in Fort Myers, Florida. It provides a continuing summer school program for Seminole Indian children. Besides helping elementary school children achieve proficiency in reading and math, this partnership provides benefits to Seminoles in building teaching skills. It also provides FGCU education students with cross-cultural teaching experience. In addition, the program incorporates Seminole culture, develops mentoring partnerships, and promotes the Language Experience Approach.

The project fulfills an important goal from the FGCU mission statement, which calls for collaboration with culturally diverse people in projects and to participate in projects in the communities it serves. It is also in tune with the education philosophy of the Seminole Tribe of Florida, Inc., which is interested in educational programs that enhance individuals' awareness of their tribal identity and that also promote their ability to function in the larger U.S. society. The Tribe also encourages self-sufficiency among its members by helping them attain quality education. This essay describes the history, budget, methods, and results of the partnership that has offered learning "beyond the walls."

BACKGROUND

A summer school program was started in 1994 at the Brighton Reservation in Glades County, Florida, to provide reading and math tutorials for elementary Native American children and to develop remedial skills important to success in local public schools during the regular school year. The program offered low teacher-to-student ratios and worked effectively with the local public school system. Sr. Mary Elizabeth Lagoy, a Roman Catholic nun, originally established and maintained the program with other sisters in her order. Since the inception of the program, in addition to Sr. Lagoy's availability for tutoring during the school year, the average grade for all elementary school Indian students increased by 0.5 to 0.9 of a grade point in the years following the first summer schools. The nuns taught without compensation as part of their church ministry. Soon after its inception the program included all Indian students at the Brighton reservation, not just those needing extra help. By 1998 Sr. Lagoy had been transferred out of the state and was not replaced. Following her departure, Louise Gopher, the Seminole Education Director at Brighton and the Parent Advisory Committee (PAC), approached Dr. Susan Stans, anthropologist and faculty member at FGCU, and asked her to continue the program.

After accepting the position, Stans met with Gopher to revise the program. They began by planning how to recruit committed and talented teachers willing to spend two weeks at the reservation. They wanted to include the Seminole culture in the curriculum and to give more substantial roles to the Seminole aides who had been hired in the past to help the teachers. The PAC approved plans throughout the process and was an integral part of carrying out the program. The PAC also selected the new name, *Emahakv Vpelofv*, which refers to the palm hammock in which Seminole children traditionally learned to carry on the customs of their people.

Stans submitted grant proposals to three private foundations to cover expenses and pay a stipend to teachers. Funding was requested for three years, a period of time deemed necessary to assess the program by tracking individual and grade-level performance during the regular school term. A private foundation funded the first year, and the second year was funded by Jack Smith Jr., the Seminole council representative from Brighton. A three-year commitment was important to building interest and skills of Seminole aides and staff. If the enrichment program is successful at the end of that period, then Seminole individuals would have the experience and knowledge to continue administering the project on their own.

BUDGET ITEMS

The proposal requested a $13,668.52 annual budget for three years, with a 3 percent cost-of-living increase the second and third years, for a total of $42,248.03. The total in-kind contribution from the Seminole Tribe and FGCU was $58,003.66. Indirect costs were calculated at 40 percent of the other personnel services.

The Seminole Tribe paid the cost of employing the four Seminole aides at a standard rate of $8 per hour for sixteen hours of workshop and seventy-two hours of teaching ($2,900). Other in-kind contributions funded one-month salaries for two education counselors, three weeks for one Seminole culture teacher, and two weeks for one Seminole library aide. Including fringe benefits, the total in-kind salary contributions from the tribe came to $15,660.

The grant budget for the four FGCU students was figured at the same rate as the aides ($8 per hour for sixteen hours of workshop and seventy-two hours of teaching). Stans was paid a flat salary ($4,167) for an estimated one month of preparation, hiring, coordination, and supervision. The figure was based on one month of her nine-month annual salary. Fringe benefits were calculated only for the director based on 32 percent of her salary (a total of $1,333).

The cost of mentoring training by Michelle Pescatrice of the School District of Lee County was based on a school-board professional rate of $28.72 per hour for six hours preparation, eight hours visitation to the Seminole reservation, and six hours presenting the workshop (a total of $574.40). Training in the Language Experience Approach was provided by an FGCU faculty member, Charleen Olliff, as part of her service hours to the university. The FGCU education advisors for the grant were considered as providing in-kind contributions from the university because of their twelve-month contracts. They were involved in the planning, recruitment, and evaluation of the project.

The only supplies requested through the grant were textbooks for the eight student teachers and aides (a total of $296.40). The texts used covered techniques of mentoring (Bellm, Whitebook, and Hnatuik 1997) and Seminole culture (Garbarino 1972). Other expenses were absorbed as institutional support from FGCU and the Seminole Tribe of Florida.

Travel funds were necessary because of the 174-mile round trip from the university to the reservation. Because this distance precluded a daily commute, FGCU students and the director carpooled to the workshop orientation on the reservation using the university van (approximately $50 in-kind). Seminole aides visiting FGCU for mentoring training used Seminole transportation ($50 in-kind). The sum of $302.76 (three cars carpooling at 0.29 cents per mile for 174 miles round trip for two trips) was requested for the FGCU students and the director to drive to the reservation each Sunday night and drive home at the end of the week. There are no motels on or near the reservation, so the PAC located homes to accommodate the group. Because of the trust status of the reservation, there are a few unoccupied furnished homes belonging to absentee owners. The PAC approached those owners, who agreed to allow three students to stay in one home, and the director and one student in another. The owners received as rent a total of $750 ($150 per occupant). This lodging arrangement cost less than two motel rooms for nine nights. Finally, the travel budget was enhanced by $756 to accommodate $21 per diem for nine days for the FGCU students while they were on the reservation.

The PAC provided $200 for toys and educational items to be used as incentives for completion of work, skill attainment, and behavior rewards, an additional $200 for supplies, and $550 for tee-shirts (given to everyone in the program) featuring designs made by the children themselves. The cost of a cook and groceries to provide each student with a hot meal each day was provided by the Brighton council representative, Jack Smith Jr. Alex Johns, the Brighton board representative, provided the meat for the end-of-school celebration dinner. The PAC provided the side dishes.

The budget for the previous year's summer school included expenses neither for the teaching nuns nor for meals; the new budget seemed, by contrast, to be appropriate to recruit student teachers, pay an outside director, and add meals and training workshops. The program would have one less week of classes but would be at the same level of intensity because of the longer school day. This schedule was a better fit for the student teachers and other employees.

THE PROGRAM SCHEDULE

In February and March of 1999, fliers and e-mail notices went out to FGCU education students regarding the open positions, which would include an immersion experience of living on the reservation for two weeks in tribal members' homes. Approximately ten people applied and six were interviewed. The education faculty recommended students who were selected for their respect for cultural differences and with consideration for their academic record and other internship experience. Louise Gopher notified potential Seminole aides or co-teachers about positions. The Seminoles were not required to have more than a high-school education, but they did have to demonstrate a willingness to learn and to teach. Four student teachers and four Seminole co-teachers were hired. Students received texts on mentoring six weeks prior to training.

Two full days were set aside for training during the week before summer school classes actually began. The first workshop session provided training in peer mentoring and in the Language Experience Approach. The second day was taken up by a visit by the FGCU students to the Brighton reservation. This cultural training was provided by the Seminole education staff. The teachers were coached on keeping journals, planning lessons, and goal setting. Goal setting with measurable objectives is important for evaluation of the program as well as for their personal growth as teachers. They were matched with partners and chose to be responsible for a specific age group during the session. Daily evaluations consisted of afternoon discussion of the day's events and journal keeping. There were parent, staff, and student assessments conducted at the end of the two-week program.

MENTORING: EVERYONE HAS SOMETHING
TO TEACH AND SOMETHING TO LEARN

Mentoring occurs when an older or more experienced individual commits herself to prepare a younger or less experienced individual in preparing and executing any life task. In the Teaching Hammock, mentoring occurred between Seminole students (those who finished their work early gained confidence and an enhanced self-image by mentoring younger students) and between the Seminole aides and the FGCU students. Elementary students mentor each other in reading and math, and

Seminole and FGCU teachers mentor each other in cultural knowledge and teaching skills. The Seminole aides mentor the FGCU students in their culture and values. FGCU education students gain practical experience in cross-cultural teaching.

The more experienced university education students model ideal teaching strategies for Seminole aides. The latter, although not licensed professional teachers, developed competencies in teaching and tutoring. They also gained knowledge about course content, thereby becoming more self-confident and more competent in interpreting education in terms of their culture. As partnered teachers, Seminole aides and FGCU student teachers planned, executed, and evaluated the lesson plans. Partnered training emphasizes trust, appreciation of both cultures, respect for each other's values, and modeling teaching behavior. This program may spur them to complete an education program or to study toward certification as Child Development Associates (CDAs). In 1998 the community had no certified native teachers. Because they were also parents, the aides also gained skills needed to guide their own children's education.

LANGUAGE EXPERIENCE APPROACH

The Language Experience Approach (LEA) mimics the traditional Seminole method of learning by observation, participation, and repetition. The children hear traditional stories or instructions from a tribal speaker, ask questions, visualize and use the material, and make measurements or other appropriate tasks. After the speaker leaves, the children retell the event, individually or in groups. They then write a story themselves or in a group; sometimes they dictate the story to the teacher. The story is edited, with the teacher helping with the principles of good grammar, content, punctuation, and spelling. By adding pictures, the story becomes a book that can be read to other children. One group took its stories to the senior lunch program and read them to the elders.

The stories can be used as math problems if the taking of measurements or the use of estimated numerical equivalents can be worked into the narrative. The children or teachers are asked to make up math problems that can be solved with grade-appropriate skills. After visiting the tribe's turtle farm, for example, they estimated money earned per pound from the sale of a six-pound turtle. Because the process of calculating math problems has been added to the public school standardized tests, students are encouraged to think about how to work through problems. When selling a single turtle, how do you determine its weight? How much is it per pound? How do you figure the total price of the turtle? What if you sold six turtles?

IMPORTANCE OF CULTURE

Several authors (Barnhardt 1991; Dauenhouer 1982; Deloria 1991; Hampton 1989; Kawagley 1995; Reyner, Lee, and Gabbard 1993; Wax, Wax, and Dumont 1989) have written about the discrepancy between formal Western educational methods and traditional Native American learning. A report on Native American drop-outs (Champagne 1991) demonstrates that students leave school because they are bored, find school irrelevant, and have difficulty interacting with other students and school personnel. The LEA approach was designed to make students' home environment relevant to concepts presented in public schools. New strategies demonstrated the relevance of education to their culture, thereby enhancing the value of education and encouraging Seminole students to remain in school through graduation. Because the Seminole students are a small part of the minority component of local schools, their need for cultural expression and intensive skill-building is not always appropriately addressed in those schools. The summer program offered an opportunity to test culturally integrated teaching methods beyond the traditional classroom setting, the better to develop the potential of Seminole students.

Adult participants learned about the culture through the ethnography (Garbarino 1972), which all were assigned to read. Moreover, Stans was able to provide insights into educational history, issues, and students at Brighton because she had lived on the reservation for twenty months beginning in 1994. She had developed networks among tribal members, worked as a liaison between Okeechobee County schools and the Brighton Education Department, and conducted her dissertation research at Brighton. As part of the training, Louise Gopher and her assistant, Diane Smith, introduced all adult participants to the distinctively Seminole world view and value system. This training was held on the reservation to provide the FGCU students with an orientation to the community before beginning to work there.

Cultural features were introduced to the children during the school through visual, audible, and experiential activities. Seminoles made presentations regarding different aspects of their culture. Children studied a *chickee*, a traditional house, from beneath its cover while a Seminole builder described how he used math to create the structure. The children examined the shapes, counted rectangles, measured the posts and crossbeams, and discussed solving problems such as how to make an even roof when the cypress logs used for crossbeams are tapered. On another occasion they wandered through the woods looking for medicinal herbs described by a Seminole elder. They collected specimens and learned the Creek words for the plants. They heard another elder speak in her native language about the days before concrete block housing; Louise Gopher translated her talk. The children also learned about early forms of transportation, cooking, gathering, the home camp, and contact with outsiders. Another woman told of the distant past, early culture, and Seminole heroes. Yet another man took the children to the old schoolhouse grounds. He pointed out features and showed pictures to help them imagine how the school looked before it was torn down. The children were fascinated with the school's concrete bowling alley that they found partially buried by the weeds. Two energetic older women taught the children the words to a song that they had played when they were children. They took everyone out under the trees to play the game used for learning Creek words.

THE CURRICULUM

The curriculum was based on appropriate learning goals, objectives, and measurable assessments. Each teacher received the list of goals when hired. The teachers were asked in addition to set their own teaching goals, and at the end of the program they evaluated both the program and their own performance. The general outline was as follows:

Goal I: to improve the education potential for Seminole Indian elementary students
  Objective 1: improve reading skills
    Assessment 1: read a minimum of two books per week
  Objective 2: improve writing skills
    Assessment 2: write about a minimum of two books per week
  Objective 3: improve math skills and describe the process

Assessment 3: compute a minimum of four word problems per week and explain the process
Objective 4: provide skill-building for promotion to next grade
Assessment 4: use drills and measures prescribed by local public school for each individual
Objective 5: develop peer mentors among the children
Assessment 5: practice reading to another student a minimum of two times per week
Objective 6: improve goal-setting and organization
Assessment 6: students write goals with help of teachers and keep portfolios to show their progress; students evaluate progress at end of session
Objective 7: improve self-esteem
Assessment 7: students take a self-esteem indicator at beginning and end of session
Goal II: to have Seminole aides and FGCU students gain competencies
Objective 1: practice goal-setting and evaluation
Assessment 1: aides and FGCU student teachers write goals, keep a journal of the experience, and evaluate their performance at the end
Objective 2: practice partnered teaching using new techniques
Assessment 2: student teachers and aides plan daily curriculum together and discuss their weaknesses and strengths at the end of the day
Goal III: for FGCU students to acquire cross-cultural teaching experience
Objective 1: keep a journal record of actions and reactions to working in a different culture
Assessment 1: summarize progress from journals at the end of the session
Goal IV: to develop nontraditional methods of classroom learning and culturally appropriate curriculum in the community setting
Objective 1: practice peer mentoring
Assessment 1: student teachers and aides keep journals from training through the experience; partners exchange journals and/or advisors evaluate beginning and ending entries
Objective 2: gain language experience

       Assessment 2: students display their work or present material
       at celebration at end of session
    Objective 3: experience cultural integration
       Assessment 3: native speakers provide information on culture
       to stimulate related activities
    Objective 4: practice goal-setting
       Assessment 4: student teachers and aides formulate personal
       goals and objectives during workshop and evaluate their
       achievement at end of session

After incorporating the general program objectives into their own teaching goals, the teachers set up the sequence of activity during the day. Both teachers and children wrote behavioral expectations on the first day.

All children gathered in one room at 9:00 every morning; they recited the Pledge of Allegiance, and one teacher provided a group activity (a song, game, or science experiment). Then the students separated into different rooms to begin their math, writing, reading, language, or craft module. The groups took turns visiting the culture classroom where they studied the Creek language and made Seminole patchwork, guided by the culture education staff. All activities included some form of art work. If a teacher had a particularly good idea, it would be shared with the other teachers. Points were given for behavior, completion of material, attendance, and general excellence; these points were used to buy incentive prizes at the end of the week. Lunch was served at 11:30 each day, and after lunch there would be either a guest speaker or a field trip. The children departed at 3:00.

EVALUATIONS

After the children left, the teachers met with the director to discuss both successes and setbacks. The daily "decompression" meetings became the primary means of solving problems as they arose and checking adherence to objectives. Everyone had an opportunity to suggest ways of dealing with perceived problems. The FGCU students could also check with the Seminole teachers and staff about culturally appropriate behavior. After each of these sessions, the director summarized the discussion in writing and handed out copies the following day as a guide to the teachers. On one occasion, an elementary teacher from central Florida visited and performed an external evaluation. After observing the teaching styles, she shared her notes with the teachers.

At the end of the program it was determined that the eight co-teachers met an average of 79 percent of the program goals. Among their comments were the need for more time to plan for the next day, although they felt that the discussion time in the afternoon was important. All of the teachers expressed a desire to return the following year. There was also some sentiment in favor of extending the program by a week, although it won't be possible to institute this modification until the program as currently constituted is further tested.

Parents and staff were asked to write their evaluations of the program from their observation of children's daily enthusiasm and their assessment of the display of work at the Celebration Day. The reactions were positive, and it was decided to continue the program as it exists for at least another year.

Three months after the program ended, the elementary students were interviewed at their school and asked specific questions about their experience. Only fourteen of the attendees could be reached, but of those, 93 percent said they would attend the summer school again. One girl was undecided between summer school and the recreation program on the reservation. When asked if they would encourage a friend to attend, 93 percent said they would do so. All the students felt that the school had helped them. Some of their comments included: "It helped me learn more." "It helped with my weak subjects." "I improved my grades." "It helped me get ready for school." Others noted especially that they had been helped in math and reading. One young girl felt the program helped her get into the highest level reading group for the first time. To an open-ended question about all the things they liked about the summer program, 24 percent replied that it was "fun." Several of them even agreed with the teachers in wanting the summer school to be extended by a week.

WEAKNESSES

The teachers, staff, and the director identified several weaknesses pertaining to meeting goals, training, the curriculum, time, and space. The use of self-learning goals needs to be strengthened and reinforced. No age-appropriate self-esteem measure was found. There was confusion regarding writing new personal goals in addition to accepting the general program goals. Some of the children were too young to write goals on their own or did not have the time at the end to examine what they had accomplished. Journaling was time-consuming albeit successful for those who kept up the practice; however, most teachers did not want to work in the evening on journals, preferring to participate in community activities. Peer mentoring among the elementary students could have been more frequent. More emphasis on using cultural experience in writing and math is needed. The use of math was the weakest part of incorporating the culture, although a few examples were developed that could be re-used next year. Developing this aspect of the program should be a priority in future sessions.

The teachers all agreed that training in classroom management would be a welcome addition to the workshop; in response, plans call for the workshop to be extended to three days to include this topic. The FGCU teachers who had participated in some kind of classroom internship prior to joining this program were highly successful at organizing their groups; those with less experience, however, would certainly benefit from additional training.

There were unavoidable scheduling problems due to unanticipated events and the necessity of dealing with children who arrived early or needed to stay late. Time to confer with parents also needed to be built into the schedule. Lack of adequate space often detracted from the focus of the work and caused confusion. For example, the four groups had to switch rooms to be near the sewing machines to make patchwork. One class was held in the entryway.

STRENGTHS

The strengths of the first session of the revised summer school program were mostly in the area of teaching techniques, use of the culture, and the culminating experience of the Celebration Day. All the teachers had bonded as a team by the end of the session and were sad to be departing. The co-teacher/mentor approach had worked so well that half-way through the session the FGCU teachers announced that they did not want their partners to be called aides but teachers, just like themselves. The Seminole teachers gained in confidence. One of them remarked in her journal, "Today was a good day. . . . [My co-teacher] was out sick today, and I was worried about teaching by myself, but once I got started there was no stopping me. I kept [the children] working hard and they kept me busy also."

The FGCU students earned the respect of the Seminole teachers, one of whom said, "The teachers from the college are very professional-like, smart, helpful, and easy to get along with. I know that what they have learned here, they will use in their future as teachers or the knowledge they learned, they'll share with others. Because I know that I sure will!"

The FGCU students brought energy, freshness, and enthusiasm to teaching, factors that outweighed their relative lack of classroom experience. They practiced their newly discovered activities with confidence and expected their co-teachers to be teachers as well. They shared readily and supported one another in a way that allowed them to share new skills. During the daily after-school meetings, they collaborated by offering thoughtful critiques, empathy for mistakes, alternative schemes for group management, peer coaching, and praise for jobs well done. They engaged in building skills in problem-solving, collaborating, incorporating diversity, and being flexible. Their evaluations proved an invaluable tool for improving the program.

The FGCU students participated after class in rodeo practice, a birthday party, and an athletic awards program. While they were thus learning about Seminole culture and heritage, some of the Seminole teachers were able to learn new things or reinforce cultural practices that had faded from memory. Several of the children cited learning about their culture and heritage as being the most important part of the program. Both children and adults were able to learn native words and songs, and since most of the young people on the reservation do not speak Creek, this reinforcement is critical to an increase in the desire to learn the language.

A final major strength of the program was Celebration Day. Every participant received tee-shirts from the PAC to wear that day. Throughout the day, the community could see the children's efforts on display. Community members were given sheets of questions to ask the students about what they had learned. Students had a chance to verbalize their experience. Seeing all the material before them allowed them to take pride in their accomplishments and draw attention to their efforts. When community members filled out the sheets saying they had visited each child's display, they were given tickets for a raffle. After a lunch under the oak hammock, teachers were introduced to the community with their students. Prizes were awarded through the raffle drawing. The *Seminole Tribune* photographer took pictures and wrote a story to honor the day. The benefit of Celebration Day was the pride of a job well done by all.

SUMMARY

In summary, the Seminole community and the university considered the partnership a success and expressed a desire to continue the program and expand it to other reservation communities. The program met its objectives in mentoring, in developing the LEA, and in cultural incorporation. The program was a success because of new friendships, the opportunity for learning, the cross-cultural exchange, and the young students' perceptions of a positive learning experience.

The community, the tribe, the PAC, the education staff, the co-teachers, the faculty, advisors, and trainers were commended for their commitment, participation, resources, and support of this partnership. By the end of the program all had experienced friendships, fun, and fatigue—and all were eager to participate again.

NOTE

1. E-ma-ha-kv V-pe-lo-fv as broken into syllables. It is pronounced ee-mah-HAH-guh uh-pee-LO-fuh. The Seminoles at Brighton call their language Creek and recognize it as a variant of the Mvskoke language spoken in Oklahoma.

REFERENCES

Barnhardt, R. 1991. Two Cultures, One School: St. Mary's, Alaska. *Canadian Journal of Native Education* 17(2):54–66.

Bellm, D., M. Whitebook, and P. Hnatuik. 1997. *The Early Childhood Mentoring Curriculum: A Handbook for Mentors*. Washington, D.C.: National Center for the Early Childhood Work Force.

Champagne, Duane. 1991. *American Indian/Alaska Native Drop-out Study*. Detroit: Gale Research.

Dauenhouer, R. 1982. *Conflicting Visions in Alaskan Education*. Fairbanks: Center for Cross-Cultural Studies, University of Alaska.

Deloria, Vine, Jr. 1991. *Indian Education in America: Eight Essays by Vine Deloria, Jr.* Boulder, Colo.: American Indian Science and Engineering Society.

Garbarino, Merwyn. 1972. *Big Cypress: A Changing Seminole Community.* Prospect Heights, Ill.: Waveland.

Hampton, E. 1989. *Towards a Redefinition of American Indian/Alaska Native Education.* Ph.D. dissertation, Harvard University.

Kawagley, A. Oscar. 1995. *A Yupaiq Worldview.* Prospect Heights, Ill.: Waveland.

Reyner, J., H. Lee, and D. Gabbard. 1993. A Specialized Knowledge Base for Teaching American Indian and Alaska Native Students. *Tribal College: Journal of American Indian Higher Education* 4(4):26–32.

Wax, M. L., R. H. Wax, and R. V. Dumont. 1989. *Formal Education in an American Indian Community: Peer Society and the Failure of Minority Education.* Prospect Heights, Ill.: Waveland.

Contributors

Margaret C. Bender is Assistant Professor of Anthropology at Wake Forest University. She teaches courses in linguistic and cultural anthropology, gender studies, Native American studies, the anthropology of education, and anthropological theory. Her research has focused on the relationship between language and culture in a variety of contexts, from Cherokee medicinal practice to family literacy education in Chicago.

Betty J. Duggan earned the doctorate in anthropology from the University of Tennessee in 1998 and then completed a certificate in museum studies at Harvard University. During 1999–2000 she held a postdoctoral academic appointment as Hrdy Visiting Research Curator at the Peabody Museum of Archaeology and Ethnology at Harvard University and currently holds a Peabody Museum Traveling Fellowship, both in support of her research on traditional Southeastern Indian basketry and basketweavers. She has been a lecturer at the University of Tennessee, consultant for numerous public humanities projects, and has published on anthropological, folklife, and archaeological topics for professional, agency, and lay audiences. She has conducted ethnographic, public history, and folklife fieldwork in Eastern Cherokee, Chitimacha, and southern Appalachian communities.

Frederic W. Gleach is a historical anthropologist working in Native North America, Puerto Rico, and Cuba. He earned his doctorate from the University of Chicago in 1992 and has taught at De Paul, Transylvania, and Cornell Universities. His first book, *Powhatan's World and Colonial Virginia: A Conflict of Cultures*, was published by the University of Nebraska Press in 1997. He is currently Society for the Humanities Fellow at Cornell, working on touristic representations of Cuba and Puerto Rico; he is also a member of the Centennial Executive Commission of the American Anthropological Association and is preparing a collection of the works of Frank Speck and his students on the Powhatan Indians.

Louise Gopher graduated from Florida Atlantic University with a major in business. She is employed as the Brighton Education Coordinator for the Seminole Tribe of Florida on its reservation near Okeechobee, Florida. She has served on the Board of Directors for the Florida Historical Society, the Ah-tah-thi-ki Museum, and the Florida Folk Life Council.

Jason Baird Jackson is Assistant Curator of Ethnology at the Sam Noble Oklahoma Museum of Natural History and Assistant Professor of Anthropology at the University of Oklahoma. He has collaborated with the Euchee (Yuchi) Tribe of Indians since 1993. He is the author of a forthcoming book on Yuchi ceremonial life to be published by the University of Nebraska Press. He is currently undertaking a regional study of music and dance among the Woodland Indian communities of eastern Oklahoma.

Lisa J. Lefler is a research associate in the Department of Anthropology at Wake Forest University and an Adjunct Assistant Professor in the Department of Sociology and Anthropology at Western Carolina University. She is also a charter board member of the Native Wellness and Healing Institute and the Native Wellness Society of Norman, Oklahoma. She is a medical and applied anthropologist who has been working with American Indian communities on a variety of research topics. She is currently working with addiction counselors who treat American Indian adolescents while continuing her research on American Indian fatherhood.

Patricia Barker Lerch is Professor of Anthropology at the University of North Carolina at Wilmington. Her research interests include pow-wows and identity, the ethnohistory of Indians in North Carolina, tourism, and religion.

Brett Riggs earned his doctorate in anthropology from the University of Tennessee. He is currently an archaeologist for the Eastern Band of Cherokee Indians and has been conducting research with, by, and for the Cherokees for more than ten years.

Donald Shannon earned his B.A. and M.A. in anthropology from Washington State University. His M.A. thesis was based on the behavioral and cultural patterns of early infant care among the Aka, a group of tropical forest foragers in the western Congo basin. He conducted fieldwork on fatherhood among the Chickasaw of south central Oklahoma in 1999 and worked as a consultant for the Chickasaw Nation in the spring of 2000. In the fall of 2000 he returned to the Central African Republic to carry out fieldwork among the Aka.

Susan E. Stans graduated from the University of Florida in 1964 with a degree in political science. She received a degree in anthropology from the University of Central Florida in 1987 and applied to graduate school at the University of Florida in anthropology. In 1994 she began her twenty-month dissertation residency at the Brighton Seminole Reservation at Okeechobee, Florida, living with a Seminole elder, Alice Snow, and received her doctorate in anthropology in 1996. Her dissertation was based on the Brighton Seminoles' attitudes about alcohol use. She has taught as an adjunct professor at the University of Central Florida and Rollins College. She was appointed Visiting Professor at Florida Gulf Coast University in February 1998. Since that time she has become Assistant Professor of Anthropology. Her appointment is through a partial grant from the Seminole Tribe of Florida, which allows her to teach half-time and to spend the other half of her time as mentor to Seminole students and university liaison to the Seminole education department. She currently conducts the summer school program, *Emahakv Vpelofv*, at the Brighton Reservation. Her current interests are native education and traditional medicine. The University Press of Florida will publish *Healing Plants: Medicine of the Florida Seminole Indians* by Stans and Alice Snow in the spring of 2001.

Russell G. Townsend is a graduate student in anthropology at the University of Tennessee. A member of the Cherokee Nation, he is particularly interested in issues of curation and interpretation of American Indian culture. Formerly a curator at the Sequoyah Museum at Fort Louden, Tennessee, he is finishing his Ph.D. and hopes to secure a position that allows him to continue his work in partnered research and museum curation.

Willard Walker is Professor Emeritus of Anthropology at Wesleyan University. His research interests in the linguistic anthropology and ethnohistory of Indian Americans have centered on the Zunis, Cherokees, and Passamaquoddies. He is currently at work on an anthropology of Cherokee texts with translations, morphemic analyses, historical background, and cultural context.